A HEAVEN FOR ANIMALS

A HEAVEN FOR ANIMALS

A Catholic Case and Why It Matters

CHRISTOPHER STECK, SJ

GEORGETOWN UNIVERSITY PRESS / WASHINGTON, DC

Cataloging-in-Publication data is on file with the Library of Congress.

978-1-64712-613-1 (hardcover)
978-1-64712-614-8 (paperback)
978-1-64712-615-5 (ebook)

∞ This paper meets the requirements of ANSI/NISO Z39.48-1992 (Permanence of Paper).

26 25 9 8 7 6 5 4 3 2 First printing

EU GPSR Authorized Representative
LOGOS EUROPE, 9 rue Nicolas Poussin,
17000, LA ROCHELLE, France
Email: Contact@logoseurope.eu

Printed in the United States of America

Cover design by TG Design
Interior design by Westchester Publishing Services

For anyone who's loved an animal and hopes to see it again.

CONTENTS

Acknowledgments ix

Introduction 1

PART I: PRELUDE TO THE ARGUMENT

1. The Catholic Tradition on Animals 9

Humans and Their Companion Animals 10

Thomas Aquinas on Animals 12

Updating Aquinas's Approach to Animals 16

Catholic Views of Animals during the Modern Period (ca. 1500–1950) 20

Conclusion 24

2. Context for Change 27

The Environmental Crisis 28

Animal Theodicy and Evolution 29

Science and Animals 32

The Minority Tradition 36

Conclusion 40

PART II: A CATHOLIC CASE FOR ANIMALS IN HEAVEN

3. The Bible on Animals 47

The *Imago Dei*: Humanity as Unique and Uniquely Responsible for Creation 48

Humanity's Dominion over Animals 50

The Fall and Its Consequences for Animals 51

The Covenant and Animals 53

The Bible and God's Plan for Animals 55

Conclusion 62

4. Contemporary Magisterial Views of Animals and Their Salvation 66
Vatican II's Cosmic Eschatology 67
Magisterial Teachings on Animals between Vatican II and *Laudato Si'* 69
Detour: Salvation by Proxy? 70
Pope Francis's *Laudato Si'* and Animal Salvation 75
The *Catechism* on Animals 78
Conclusion 81

PART III: CONSTRUCTING A CATHOLIC THEOLOGY OF ANIMALS

5. A Trinitarian Theology of Animal Salvation 87
Animal Salvation in a Trinitarian Context 88
The Holy Spirit as Salvific Bond 92
The Church's Prayer for Salvation: Animals Included 96
Conclusion 100

6. Animals in Heaven 104
Nature and Grace 105
Critiques of Animals in Heaven 107
Animals in Heaven: A Sketch 111
Conclusion 118

PART IV: THE IMPLICATIONS FOR HOW WE TREAT ANIMALS

7. Animal Ethics: Theory 125
Philosophical Approaches to Animal Ethics 126
Catholic Ethics 129
The Kingdom of God 132
Animals and the Already / Not Yet of the Kingdom 135
The Vocation of the Christian: A Universal and Personal Calling 138
Conclusion 140

8. Animal Ethics: Applied 143
Principles for Animal Ethics 144
Eating Meat from Factory Farms 148
Using Animals in Experiments 153
Conclusion 157

Postscript: The Ambassador Dog 161

Index 167

About the Author 177

ACKNOWLEDGMENTS

This book both continues and develops the arguments of *All God's Animals: A Catholic Theological Framework for Animal Ethics* (Georgetown University Press) but now in a form that is, I hope, accessible to a broader, nonacademic audience. It follows that all those who helped make that earlier book possible also deserve credit here, including, among others, the Jesuits of Grand Coteau, LA; Otto Hentz, SJ and Brian McDermott, SJ; Nancy and Kevin Clark; and David Clough.

The challenge of writing this book was significantly eased by Georgetown University Press's decision to publish it. Their decision meant not only that I'd be working with a press already familiar to me but also that I'd be able to avoid copyright issues that might have otherwise arisen in using material from the earlier book. My thanks to Al Bertrand and the team at GUP for their enthusiasm and support for this project.

I'm also indebted to the Thomas J. Healey family. I have the good fortune to occupy the chair endowed by them—the Thomas J. Healey Family Distinguished Professor in Ethical Studies—and it has provided me with critical support for the research, writing, and publication of this book.

Colleagues reviewed the manuscript and helped improve its arguments. Christine Trotter reviewed the discussions of the Bible and animals in chapter 3, while David Cloutier did the same for the two chapters on ethics (namely, 7 and 8). I asked Eugene Schlesinger to bring his expertise on Balthasar to chapter 5, and, fortunately for me, he ended up reading the entire manuscript. The anonymous reviewers for Georgetown University Press gave excellent feedback. Dawn Sjurset provided special assistance with an early section of the book. I'm deeply grateful to all these individuals for the improvements they made possible. Any remaining errors are, of course, entirely on me.

The excellent students in my "Dogs and Theology" class (fall 2023) merit a round of applause. They were required to slog through a *very* early version of the manuscript and, in doing so, provided a great sample group for assessing the text's clarity.

Finally, one other group deserves a special thanks: all those who, though not immersed in theology or familiar with its peculiar terminology, intrepidly endeavored to get through the previous book. Kudos to them for their valiant labor; it furthered my determination to craft a work more easily digestible for all (on that score, a special shoutout to Bill Lic).

Christopher Steck, SJ
Jesuit Community
Georgetown University
September 1, 2025
World Day of Prayer for the Care of Creation

Introduction

If the story is to be believed, St. Robert Bellarmine allowed bugs to bite him. When asked why, he responded: "We shall have heaven to reward us for our sufferings. But these poor creatures have nothing but the enjoyment of the present life."[1] I imagine the story is fictional, but its traction in Catholic circles testifies to an instinct of Catholic piety common throughout the centuries. Catholics have cherished stories like Bellarmine and his bugs because they recount deeds they expect of their saints—treating animals with Christlike compassion.

A different strand in the Catholic tradition, however, developed alongside this pious esteem for saintly compassion. It is more intellectual and defined by what has been the mainstream approach for much of Catholic history: By God's design, animals have a duty to serve us and give us joy. We can use them, even cause them suffering, as long as we have a good reason for doing so.

As we will see in the chapters ahead, there is a tension here between saintly compassion for animals and a rationally justified use of them—one that has recurred throughout Catholicism's long history. Pope Francis has charted a new path in negotiating this tension. His views on the natural world and the creatures within it are not revolutionary—they have their basis in the teachings of the Second Vatican Council (1962–65) and the writings of popes John Paul II and Benedict XVI. But he has shifted Catholic thought toward the more animal-friendly strand of the tradition. One effect of that shift is an encouragement that animals will, in some manner or form, join us in the age to come.

In the chapters that follow, I aim to make a Catholic case for that hope. Though I continue many of the arguments found in my earlier work, *All God's Animals: A Catholic Theological Framework for Animal Ethics* (Georgetown University Press, 2019), this book updates those arguments and conveys them in a way that serves, I hope, a general audience. The sources for many of this book's claims can be found in *All God's Animals,* so readers interested in digging deeper or going further will want to refer to that work.

The primary goals of this book are, first, to present a systematic, theological argument that heaven will include at least some of the animals of the present age, and then, second, to explore the ethical implications of that view. The argument for animals in heaven is based on the teachings of recent popes, biblical scholarship, and contemporary Catholic thought on Christ, the end times (eschatology), salvation, the Trinity, and the Holy Spirit. Though I understand arguments like, "We won't be happy without our companion animals," or "God's going to bring our animal friends to heaven out of love for us," those are not the arguments I pursue here. I believe that the salvation of an animal, whether a beloved dog or some animal in the wild unknown to any of us, is ultimately not a matter of human need but God's desire. And Christ has revealed what that desire is: It is "to sum up all things in Christ, in heaven and on earth" (Ephesians 1:10). If animals are to be saved, it is because they are included in this summing up. There is no special pet door or rainbow bridge to heaven that bypasses Christ.

The book argues that animals and all of creation are indeed included in the "work of Christ." With that phrase, I refer to the life, death, and resurrection of Christ and the salvation he achieved. Theologians use other phrases to convey a similar meaning. "Salvation history," for example, refers to the history of God's salvific work. It is a history that begins with creation and then continues with the call of Abraham, the formation of a chosen people led by Moses, the anointing of David as king, the collapse of the Israelite kingdom, and the announcement by the prophets of a future Messiah (the Anointed One). Christians believe Jesus Christ to be the fulfillment of that prophecy.

Other terms for God's work in Christ include the "divine economy" (i.e., God's labor in the world as recounted in the Bible) and "God's salvific plan." All of these terms—the work of Christ, salvation history, the divine economy, and God's salvific plan—are different ways of naming the basic Christian belief that God has been at work in human history, entered that history in the sending of his Son Jesus Christ, and, through Christ, now offers salvation to all human persons. I argue that God *also* includes animals in this salvific plan in ways appropriate to each animal. For some animals with developed cognition (e.g., dolphins and elephants), salvation will include, we can hope, God's resurrection of them in the end times; for other animals (e.g., fruit flies and worms), God's salvation might entail something else, such as God recreating new versions of them.

My hope is that readers will enjoy an added dividend in undertaking this foray into Catholic theology. Understanding how God might wish to save *animals* and bring them to heaven requires us to understand the theological basics of *human* salvation. The book's exercise in theology will then, I hope, offer readers a chance to deepen their understanding of the fundamentals of Catholic theology and the wonderful gift that God has achieved in Christ Jesus.

* * *

The book is divided into four parts; each part has two chapters. The first part, "Prelude to the Argument," clears out the historical underbrush and fashions the theological landscape for my case. I examine why Thomas Aquinas rejected the idea of animals in heaven and note how his position influenced Catholic views of animals up through the mid-twentieth century. Recently, however, a number of forces have converged to encourage a reconsideration of these views (e.g., the climate crisis and new insights into animals and the natural world), and I examine those in the second chapter.

The second part, "A Catholic Case for Animals in Heaven," brings us to the core of my case for animals. I argue that we find significant support in both the Bible and church teachings for what theologians call a "cosmic eschatology" (from the Greek word *eschaton*, end). A *cosmic* eschatology is committed to the view that God's salvific intent in Jesus Christ encompasses not only humanity but the whole created order, and, thus, at the end of time, the entire cosmos will join humanity and be saved in Christ.

This eschatology does not, however, necessarily mean that individual animals of the present age will be resurrected. Based on recent teachings, including those found in the writings of popes John Paul II, Benedict XVI, and Francis, I make a case, nonetheless, that at least some of these animals, those with sentience and especially those with developed cognition, will be resurrected in the age to come.

By necessity, the book's third part, "Constructing a Catholic Theology of Animals," becomes more speculative, as I attempt to make theological sense of two ideas: God saves animals, and animals will join us in heaven. The discussion needs to be speculative, even if grounded in mainstream Catholic theology, since the Church has no formal position on the two ideas. Though I defend the soundness of my theological constructions, I do not present them as *the* explanation of animal salvation or of the animals' lives in heaven. Rather, I merely intend to show that the two ideas—animals being saved and welcomed into the heavenly reign of God—are theologically sensible against detractors who reject them as absurd.

In the fourth part, "The Implications for How We Treat Animals," I explore how an animal-inclusive view of God's work in Christ impacts our ethics of animal care. I understand these ethical implications in terms of the "kingdom of God," a theme that is central to Jesus's preaching and that likewise has become important to contemporary Catholic thought. If animals are to be part of the kingdom that Christ inaugurated and whose fullness we await, then Christian treatment of animals should embody, ideally at least, the values of the kingdom (harmony, peace, kindness, etc.). Nonetheless the fullness of the kingdom awaits the Second Coming of Christ, and until then we will be required to commit acts that are at odds with kingdom values. For example, we will sometimes need to act violently to protect the innocent, whether from armed assailants or rodent intruders.

Some final notes. In the course of the book's arguments, I refer to a number of church documents. They do not all have the same level of authority. The teachings of an "ecumenical" or universal council (such as the Second Vatican Council) are distinctively authoritative, as are the formal writings of popes (e.g., their apostolic constitutions and encyclicals). However, when a pope says something in a homily, an interview, or a casual chat with visitors, it is not considered a formal teaching of the Church or of that pope. Thus while the theological views about the natural world found in Pope Francis's *Laudato Si'*, an encyclical, are considered, generally speaking, formal church teachings, a homily he gave on the Feast of St. Francis is not.

The *Catechism of the Catholic Church*, a document that I cite a number of times, was established by John Paul II's apostolic constitution *Fidei Depositum* in 1992. It is also considered authoritative, and its views are assumed to be doctrinal, if not dogmatic (i.e., unchanging theological beliefs). Documents written by the International Theological Commission (ITC) do not have the same authoritative status, but they have typically been approved by the head of the Congregation for the Doctrine of the Faith (i.e., the CDF, now renamed the Dicastery for the Doctrine of the Faith). These documents are thus seen as theologically sound albeit unofficial expressions of the Church's beliefs.

Deciding what's authoritative, and at what level, is more complicated than all this. For example, statements in official documents often need interpretation, and not all will agree on what the correct interpretation is. In addition, teachings conveyed in a lesser authoritative setting (e.g., a homily) gain indirect authority when they express and confirm formal church teaching. Many of the passages I cite from documents with less authority, such as those by the ITC, align with the teachings found in *Laudato Si'*—which, again, as an encyclical is one of the highest expressions of papal teaching. The passages cited from less authoritative writings gain a patina of formal teaching through their affinity with the theology of *Laudato Si'*.

My primary focus is on animals that are sentient. The language that scientists use to describe the inner mental states of animals is not settled, in part because we have much to learn about the inner lives of both animals and humans alike. Terms like "sentience," "consciousness," and "subjective awareness" (which is not the same as self-awareness) are not used consistently among scholars. I use "sentient" as a broad term describing those animals that have a subjective awareness, however primitive or developed, and a capacity to experience themselves as having joy or suffering pain.

By "creatures," I refer to any living thing created by God. My use of "animal" follows the traditional, though admittedly too simplified, division of the world's creatures into animals, plants, and inanimate matter; animal, as used here, thus includes not only birds and marine life but any nonplant life. It has become common in scholarly circles to use terms like "human animals" and "other-than-human animals" in order to remind us that humans are also animals. However, in order to keep my language aligned with general usage and church documents, I have kept to the traditional terminology (i.e., humans and animals).

Unless otherwise indicated, all quotations from the Bible follow the translation found in the New American Bible Revised Edition. Church documents are cited parenthetically in the text. Those documents can be found on the Vatican website: www.vatican.va.

* * *

Though the book's focus is on animals broadly, and not just pets, I will consider it at least partially successful if it brings hope to those who grieve the loss of a companion animal. My keener interest, however, is that some will find the argument that God plans to include all creatures in Christ's salvific work persuasive, not only on an intellectual level but an affective one as well. The implications of the book's case involve more than just switching doctrinal camps, moving from one intellectual position ("no, animals don't go to heaven") to another ("yes, they do"). If God's ultimate desire for the individual animals of the present age is that they join him in the next, then that belief affects and deepens the responsibilities that Christians have to care for creation and the animals within it.

In a joint statement on creation, Pope Francis and Patriarch Bartholomew (the spiritual leader of the Eastern Orthodox Church) stated that the object of prayer is "to change the way we perceive the world in order to change the way we relate to the world" ("Joint Message: World Day of Prayer for Creation," September 1, 2017).

God willing, this book will provide some small service to their plea—helping those whom God has named creation's stewards to see the nonhuman world anew and inspiring new ways of relating to it.

NOTE

1. Edward Hartpole Lecky, *History of European Morals from Augustus to Charlemagne*, vol. 2 (London: Longmans, Green, and Co., 1902), 172n3.

PART I

Prelude to the Argument

CHAPTER 1

The Catholic Tradition on Animals

The son of a colleague had a miserable first day of class. His initial enthusiasm at moving up to Catholic middle school was quashed during his religion class. Perhaps with an interest in grabbing the students' attention, the teacher of his sixth-grade religion class announced, at the start of class before any lecture had begun, that none of the students would ever see their pets in heaven. The statement, delivered with pontifical certitude, certainly succeeded in getting their attention: It left the students dismayed and one girl in tears.

The pronouncement hit my colleague's son particularly hard. His dog, a golden retriever named Sam, was beloved by his family and had been a constant in their lives through work-related displacements. Back home on that first day of class, the fourteen-year-old Sam was facing a host of medical problems, and it was clear he would not live long. The boy's heart ached, but apparently God's did not. Or so proclaimed the teacher.

Many would criticize the teacher's statement for its callousness even if they agreed with it. To be sure, she could have taken a more pastoral approach and softened the harshness of the statement. Pope Paul VI, for instance, rose to the occasion when faced with a similar circumstance. In response to a boy mourning the loss of his dog, he said: "One day we will again see our animals in the eternity of Christ." His words were ambiguous, perhaps by intent, but at least they had the virtue of not crushing a kid's heart.

There is however an additional reason to criticize the teacher's statement. It's not just pastorally bad; it's also wrong. And unfortunately it's not an uncommon mistake: Many Catholics believe that heaven's doors are closed to all animals. My goal in this chapter is to understand how this view became so widespread and note the tensions it has created, historically and in the present, within the Catholic world.

I begin first with a brief consideration of our relationships with pets in order to probe why views like the teacher's above are so unwelcomed in some Catholic quarters before turning to understand the origin of them. Among the various relationships that humans have with animals, our relations with pets are some of the most intense and fervent. For critics, this fervor approaches the idolatrous. For others, the devotion to pets is an expression of compassion's ideal. As sweeping generalizations, both are inaccurate, but they each nonetheless contain an element of truth. People's relationships with their pets take different forms, and some are better than others.

Given this diversity of practices, the pet–human relationship offers a good starting point for understanding the complexities of what it means, for us and for God, to genuinely love animals. Does a person's love for a dog reflect anything about how God loves animals and, in turn, how we are to love them? In later chapters I will argue that our care for animals should follow the divine pattern. Inasmuch as God's love includes all animals, so also should ours.

But that's for later. For now I want to look at our relationships with pets—or, using the term preferred by many, companion animals—before turning to understand Catholicism's historical resistance to granting those loving bonds any theological or salvific significance.

HUMANS AND THEIR COMPANION ANIMALS

Catholics are keenly interested in the eternal fate of their pets—understandably so, given how devoted they are to them. They often see companion animals as part of the family—planning vacations around them, including them in annual Christmas pictures, celebrating their birthdays, and ritualizing their deaths. Catholics are not, of course, alone in these practices. As a culture we have become quite enamored with our companion animals.

No affair better highlights this growing devotion than the tragedies that occurred during Hurricane Katrina in 2005. Obeying what they believed to be federal norms, rescuers refused to allow victims to bring their pets into transport vehicles (boats, helicopters, and buses). The result was that some victims made the risky choice to decline rescue in order to remain with their beloved pets. For many of them, it was a fatal decision. In the wake of the outcry that followed, Congress passed the Pets Evacuation and Transportation

Standards (PETS) Act, which authorized FEMA to provide assistance and shelter to pets and service animals in their evacuation plans.

A number of pundits in blogs and videos have addressed the growing interest among Catholics about the final destiny of animals, as any internet search for "Catholic," "pets," and "heaven" will show. Their views vary, but often they impart what they believe to be the mainstream Catholic answer (i.e., no animals in heaven or, at least, a cautiousness about the prospect) while being pastorally sensitive to their audiences' concern for their pets. The favored go-to answer in the attempt to thread this needle is to suggest that if an individual needs their pet to be happy, God will provide it to them—with the subtext being that no one will have such a need, given the joy that God's infinite beauty and goodness will bring us.

Some of these pundits, however, are more pointedly critical. The hope that animals will join us in heaven is not only wrong but is driven by an inordinate love for animals. Their criticisms are understandable given the extremes of animal care practiced by some: dressing dogs and cats in designer clothes, giving them luxurious Christmas gifts that the animals themselves cannot appreciate, laying them to rest in expensive burial plots. In my mind the award for pet excess goes to Neuticles, the polypropylene replacement testicles for dogs that have been fixed in order to restore the dog's "self-esteem." I suspect that such extravagance is what the *Catechism of the Catholic Church* has in mind when it states that it is "unworthy to spend money on [animals] that should as a priority go to the relief of human misery" (no. 2418).

Nonetheless the unfortunate excesses of some are not representative of all. In contrast to the above, countless relationships between humans and their pets are marked by a distinctive goodness and praiseworthiness. It's not only that those relationships are genuinely loving; they are also emotionally sound and healthy in how they respect the distinct, species-specific needs and wants of both parties in the relationship.[1] Dogs and cats are not treated as stand-in babies but as the animals they are.

We can go one step further. Such relationships with companion animals are not just morally legitimate but examples of what Pope Francis holds as essential to human flourishing: communion with nonhuman creatures. "The human person grows more, matures more and is sanctified more," he tells us, "to the extent that he or she enters into relationships, going out from themselves to live in communion with God, with others and *with all creatures*" (*Laudato Si'*, §240, emphasis added). Perhaps, then, God hopes that the relationships we have with companion animals will be instructive for the relationships that we are to have, when possible, with all other nonhuman creatures.

I'll return to this idea in the postscript. Here I want to understand better how we came to this muddled state where many Catholics passionately love the animals in their lives while questioning whether God does the same.

THOMAS AQUINAS ON ANIMALS

The Church has no official position on animals in heaven. There might be animals in heaven; there might not be. So how did the belief that Catholicism rules out a heaven for animals become so widespread? The short answer: the powerful influence of St. Thomas Aquinas (d. 1274).

It would be hard to exaggerate the importance of this Dominican friar for Catholic theology. The esteem he's been given is amply deserved. Aquinas assembled the riches of the Catholic tradition, harmonized Christian doctrine with the best scientific and philosophical thinking of his time, and brought together the varied commitments of Christian belief (e.g., God, Christ, salvation, and the Church) into an eminently coherent, systematic form. Perhaps no other theologian since Aquinas could presume, with justification, to pen a work with the immodest title of *Summa Theologiae* (a comprehensive summation of theology). This enormous corpus contains answers to 631 questions and, in its contemporary published form, fills five volumes comprising over 3,000 pages. Aquinas's massive output was made possible by his photographic memory and use of multiple scribes assisting him at the same time as he dictated his thoughts to each of them in turn.

Overview

This theological luminary of the Catholic tradition rejected the idea that animals and plants would join us in the age to come. Angels, humans, the heavenly spheres, and the prime elements will share in the life to come, but not dogs or dolphins, elephants or eagles, pansies or pine trees.

Before getting into the basics of Aquinas's argument, we can note with interest what was *not* significant for it: the Bible itself. Aquinas believed that human reason—the capacity that all human beings have to understand our world and draw conclusions about it (what theologians call "natural reason")—could answer the question of animals in heaven. Basically Aquinas would expect that, in principle, a diverse gathering of intelligent persons—Catholics, Protestants, Orthodox Christians, Jews, Muslims, and any person open to the idea of a spiritual world—would arrive at the same conclusion based simply on their reasoning: The animals of the present age will not be in heaven. The significance of this for our discussion is that we do not need training in theology to have an opinion about whether Aquinas is right or wrong. Each of us can agree or disagree with his conclusions by doing what Aquinas did: using our ability to reason, even if our capacity for doing so is not equal to his.

So what is Aquinas's argument? The short version is that humans have immortal souls and animals do not. And because animals do not have immortal souls, they are not able to be resurrected. The argument is not so much that God has decided against raising animals up to heaven. Rather natural reason leads us to see that *God is not able to resurrect them*, even if God wanted to do so. To go back to our initial story, God will not resurrect Sam, the grieving boy's dog, because it is impossible for God to do so.

On first glance, that might seem a silly claim to make about what an all-powerful God can or cannot do. However it makes a good deal of sense within the framework developed by Aquinas. To understand why leads us into some heavy philosophical theory about the immortal soul, much of which Aquinas adapted from Aristotle (384–322 BCE), whom Aquinas referred to simply as "the Philosopher." A foray into the theory is not an easy trek but an unavoidable one if we are to understand the traditional Catholic rejection of animals in heaven.

Aquinas, following Aristotle, held that the human person is a composite of body and soul. The soul (*anima*) is what animates, makes alive, the matter of our bodies and gives to that matter its form as a particular living human person. Until matter is animated by the soul, it is formless and has no properties or characteristics, a kind of cosmic tofu.

All living creatures have a soul: a rational soul for humans, a sensitive soul for animals, and a vegetative soul for plants. The soul takes the formless, property-less matter and forms it, activates it, into a living being. Creatures are not composed of two separate parts (the body and the soul). Rather, each creature is one composite being of body and soul.

Regarding the possibility of life after death, Aquinas argues that since the human soul is, unlike that of animals, immortal, it lives on after the body dies. In contrast, the animal, which does not have an immortal soul, ceases to exist once it dies. Again natural human reason leads us to affirm this—or at least, that is what Aquinas believed.

The Argument for the Immortality of the Human Soul

To understand Aquinas's case for the immortality of the human soul, we can begin with the observation that we humans are able to think abstractly, forming concepts that transcend the physical world. For example, we can conceive of the idea of "humanity" in the abstract without having any particular human person in mind. We can also understand basic mathematical principles (e.g., a + b = b + a) and geometric principles (e.g., the sum of the angles of a triangle is 180°) apart from perceiving a physical object.[2]

To think abstractly is to think in ways that are not entirely dependent on our bodily senses. Since we can sometimes think without relying on our bodily senses, there must be something about us, some sort of operation in us, that is *not* bodily and thus is beyond the physical. That is, our minds can function in ways that do not, at least not always, depend on physical things or on our bodily perception of those physical things. Therefore—and this is important—it must be the case that we human persons are not *entirely* bound by matter. Our thinking can sometimes work without directly relying on material things or our physical perceptions, and so there must be some dimension of us that is nonmaterial or spiritual. Again Aquinas here is mostly following ancient Greek philosophy; his argument is not based on Christian beliefs. It is simply a matter of observation and reason.

Now we come to a key step in Aquinas's argument: Since the spiritual aspect of ourselves (i.e., the human soul) does not depend on matter, we can also infer that this dimension of our identity is able to survive the death of our bodies. That is, since our spiritual selves do not depend completely on matter, they remain unaffected when the material body dies. Therefore our souls survive bodily death and are, in that sense, immortal.

We can see where this is going. Unlike humans, animals don't have what it takes intellectually to be blessed with immortal souls: the ability to think abstractly. They are instead *entirely* dependent on their bodily existence to function. Whatever they do as living creatures, whether playing, searching for food, fleeing predators, or thinking about their herd mates, is *wholly* bound by the activities of their bodies—their brains, organs, muscles, and so forth. Nothing about animals, therefore, transcends their physical bodies, and so once their bodies die, nothing of them remains. Again it is not that God refuses to resurrect Sam the golden retriever but rather that God *cannot* resurrect Sam, because after Sam dies, there's nothing left of him, no soul for God to resurrect.

Should this argument be seen as the official Catholic position? No. The Church *does* affirm that the human soul is immortal. Pope Leo X formally taught this in 1513, and it's been considered doctrine ever since. As the *Catechism of the Catholic Church* states: "The Church teaches that every spiritual soul is created immediately by God—it is not 'produced' by the parents—and also that it is immortal: it does not perish when it separates from the body at death, and it will be reunited with the body at the final Resurrection" (*Catechism*, no. 366). However the Church is *not* committed to the particular philosophical arguments that Aquinas used to defend the immortality of the human soul. More important for us, neither is the Church committed to Aquinas's statements regarding animals in heaven. Catholics can disagree with the arguments Aquinas uses to justify belief in the immortal soul and with what is a corollary of those arguments: that animals don't go to heaven because their souls are not immortal.

Aquinas's Theological Arguments against Animals in Heaven

In addition to the above philosophical argument, Aquinas offers two theological reasons for denying animals an afterlife. First, animals will have no reason to be in heaven. Their purpose is to serve humanity, but we will no longer need them in the next life. Second, life in heaven will center on the beatific vision, the direct spiritual contemplation of God. Since animals are incapable of such a vision, they will not be able to enjoy heaven.[3]

Over the next several chapters, we will see that these two theological claims have become suspect in light of contemporary teaching about animals. Regarding the first argument, recent papal teachings, particularly *Laudato Si'*, insist that animals are created by God for purposes beyond that of serving humanity. Regarding the second, we will see that statements made by Pope Francis, like his view that "the risen Christ embraces and illumines all things" (*Laudato Si'*, §83), suggest the possibility that in heaven creaturely relationships with God will take other forms than that of the beatific vision, at least as traditionally understood.

Though it is popularly believed that the Catholic Church officially rejects the idea that animals will join us in heaven, the Church actually has no formal position on the issue. Aquinas's influential rejection of animals in heaven was based primarily on the science and philosophy of his time, not on divine revelation. The specific arguments he uses against animals in heaven have no formal church support and, given recent church teachings, have become suspect.

UPDATING AQUINAS'S APPROACH TO ANIMALS

One response to Aquinas's argument against animals in heaven is just to dismiss it outright. It is human hubris, one could argue, to believe we can understand a phenomenon that defies firsthand study (i.e., death) *and* presume to know the limits of what God can and cannot do when faced with it.

I will circle back to this critique below, but for now, I want to explore a different response: Is it possible to affirm the basics of Aquinas's argument *but* do so in a way that leads to a more animal-friendly conclusion? I believe it is. Following an approach sympathetic to Aquinas, I suggest that his argument against animals in heaven is more readily applicable to a subset of creatures—those with very limited cognition such as gnats and the short-lived mayfly—but not to more cognitively sophisticated creatures.

Taking the case of less cognitively developed animals first, we can begin by asking whether it is possible for God to resurrect, say, a dead gnat. God could, of course, create an exact duplicate of that gnat, one that is the same in every physical detail as its recently deceased version. But would that copy really be the *same* gnat? It seems not. The new gnat would be merely a clone of the now dead gnat and not a true resurrection of it. Moreover, it would seem that if God wants to have that now-dead gnat in heaven, he has no other option than creating a clone since he *can't* resurrect that gnat. A gnat does not have any sort of nonbodily reality (e.g., a personal consciousness or individual subjectivity) that could provide continuity between its present version and its "resurrected" self. Nothing about a gnat at its death (e.g., a consciousness or subjectivity) could be transferred into a newly resurrected body in a way that allows us to say, "This gnat in heaven is the *same* gnat as the one that died on earth."

However, we *can* make an argument that such a continuity exists for other animals. Aquinas effectively makes abstract thinking the measure for whether continuity between this life and the next is possible, but there are other, less-exclusive markers. One such candidate is subjective awareness or sentience. The awareness of ourselves as subjects—that odd and inexplicable capacity a person has to be aware of oneself as a self, the awareness of myself as "me"—is a quality that doesn't appear entirely material and thus might be something that could transcend the death of a person's body. Yes, it is true, sentience depends on a physical substrate (i.e., the brain), but that organ and its neurons and chemicals are not, by themselves, enough to explain the experience of being a sentient subject. Sentience, then, like abstract thinking, suggests the possibility that we humans are not entirely physical beings. The same argument can be applied to animals.

First, though, a cautionary note. As I observed in the introduction, the language that scientists use to describe our inner mental states is not settled. Terms like "sentience," "consciousness," and "subjective awareness" are not used consistently, especially when applied to animals. I will use "sentient" as a broad, descriptive term for all those animals that have a subjective awareness, however primitive or developed, and a capacity to experience themselves as feeling joy or suffering pain. As I am using the term, sentience does not necessarily include self-awareness, but it does imply that the animal has at least a primitive sense of self.

From what we can tell, many animals (elephants, chimpanzees, dolphins, and, yes, dogs and cats) share with us this baffling sense of self and subjectivity. Numerous books and scientific studies have examined the rich interior lives of animals and shown their cognitive sophistication. Their findings point to the possibility that animals are not merely physical creatures but rather have some aspect (e.g., a consciousness and subjective awareness) that is more than just the chemicals and physical matter that compose their bodily selves. To use an idea popular in science fiction, we can imagine that God could "upload" a deceased dog's consciousness (with its memories, learned abilities, personality, relational bonds, affections for particular humans and other dogs, etc.) into a new and improved dog-body in heaven. God can do so in a way that would allow us to say that "this" dog in heaven is in continuity with, is the *same* as, "that" dog that just died on earth. They are genuinely the same dog since the two have the same consciousness, one that has been moved from one body to another. In contrast, it doesn't make sense to imagine that God could upload the consciousness of an amoeba into a new version of it in heaven. From what we know of an amoeba, there isn't anything about it that can be uploaded into a different body.

My point is that Aquinas might be on to something in placing limits on what kind of creature God can meaningfully raise from the dead. In order for an animal to be resurrected, we should be able to identify some sort of beyond-the-body continuity linking the previously dead creature to its resurrected form. And such a continuity doesn't seem possible between, say, a dead mayfly and a resurrected version. However, animals with a developed consciousness and a sense of self do seem to have the basis for continuity between this life and the next. Thus God can, should God choose, preserve that aspect of the animal through its resurrection. The resurrected "personhood" of that animal will be in continuity with its previous self. In heaven it will resume its existence as a particular subject, continuing its personal story, acting in ways that reflect its distinctive personality, enjoying the relationships it established on earth, and building upon its learned abilities. It will not just physically *appear* to be the previous animal; it will, in a genuine sense, *be* that once-dead animal.

And so given the range of cognitive abilities found among animals, one response to the challenge raised by Aquinas is to allow that God could grant a renewal to all animals but in a way that is appropriate to each animal's natural capacities. Sentient animals have a nonmaterial or spiritual dimension to their lives that could, with God's intervention, transcend bodily death. For such animals, we can speak meaningfully of their resurrection. Other animals like fleas and amoebas seem to lack this type of spiritual component, and so their salvation might take a different form (for example, a merely physical re-creation of their earthly bodies).

My intent in framing it this way is not to suggest that a clear demarcation separates animals that can be resurrected from those that can't. The reality is likely much more complex than an either/or. My main argument is that from what we know now, at least some animals do have what it takes—some sort of nonmaterial reality—such that God can preserve their earthly selves and bring them to heaven. God can do so in a way that those resurrected animals will genuinely be the same animals as they were on earth.

Interestingly for us, some church statements on the human soul focus on just this aspect: preserving continuity between this life and the next. Rather than the approach taken by Aristotle and Aquinas—who understood the soul as the spiritual form of matter—these statements highlight the soul's role as the guarantor of continuity. Each person has a unique personal reality that continues as the person transitions in death from the present age to their future resurrected life, and the "soul" is that reality that ensures this continuity. Without such a preserver of continuity between this life and the next, the Church maintains, we'd be talking about two different persons: the individual living in this world and their replacement in heaven. They may look and act the same, but they would in reality be two different people. For this reason, the Church holds that there must be some aspect of the person that provides an identifiable continuity between a person's temporal life in the present and its resurrected form. The soul serves this function.

Thus, for example, a document by the Congregation for the Doctrine of the Faith (CDF), "Letter on Certain Questions Concerning Eschatology" (1979), maintained "that a spiritual element survives . . . after death, an element endowed with consciousness and will, so that the 'human self' subsists [survives]. To *designate* this element [i.e., the personal identity that survives death as a consciousness and will], the Church uses the word 'soul'" (CDF,

"Letter on Certain Questions" §3, emphasis added). A 1992 document published by the Vatican's International Theological Commission (ITC), "Some Current Questions in Eschatology," likewise argues that without the soul, "God could create a person" who is "entirely equivalent" to a deceased person, "but if there is no existential continuity between the two"—if, that is, there is not some nonmaterial reality like a soul that guarantees the continuity of personal identity—"then that second person cannot be the same as the first" (ITC, "Some Current Questions in Eschatology," §4.3). Our personhood, that which makes each person the unique reality he or she is, endures after death, and the soul is the link connecting our earthly and heavenly selves.

This understanding of the soul as the marker of a person's continuity between this life and the next can be adapted to include animals. If an animal's consciousness and subjectivity are such that we can imagine a real continuity between its life in the present and its resurrected form, then perhaps we can also believe that this animal has a spiritual facet, some sort of distinctive "self," that God will choose to preserve when the animal dies. If so it is possible to modify Aquinas's argument. God could genuinely restore and resurrect at least some animals, those with subjectivity and awareness of self. However, creatures with little or no consciousness (and we can include plant life here) seem to be *entirely* physical creatures, and thus Aquinas's argument against animals in heaven would apply to them: There is nothing about them for God to resurrect once their bodies die.

I note again, however, my intent is not to draw a sharp divide between two types of animals, the cognitively sophisticated ones and those not so capable. The variety that animal cognition takes is likely too complex for such a simple division. My primary intent is only to argue that we *can* make sense of a genuine resurrection for at least some animals.

Finally, as I observed at the beginning of this section, one response to Aquinas's approach is simply to reject it altogether, arguing that it is not wise for human reason to judge what God can and cannot do, especially when dealing with the mystery of death. Perhaps human reason can stand in judgment over wonderful philosophical puzzles, like whether God can make a square circle. But reasoned reflection on the transition beyond death is different. Unlike other matters in the world that we can probe and prod with theories and hypotheses, death eludes the grasp of human reason. And if we can't claim clarity about death, then perhaps we must forgo claims about what can or cannot happen when God confronts the death of his beloved creature. Maybe God can, after all, resurrect the lowly amoeba.

CATHOLIC VIEWS OF ANIMALS DURING THE MODERN PERIOD (CA. 1500–1950)

Aquinas's views decisively shaped Catholic perspectives on animals up until the mid-twentieth century. Unfortunately, the teachings of the time were sometimes distorted by individuals desiring to use and abuse animals in order to serve human interests. It is not a particularly edifying moment in the Church's history. Fortunately, since the Second Vatican Council (1963–65), the Church has distanced itself from attitudes characteristic of that age. The fault for those attitudes does not lie so much with the teachings themselves. Contemporary Thomists (scholars whose theology is informed by Thomas Aquinas) have rightly shown that Aquinas's thought can be used effectively to respond to the environmental crisis and the need to care for animals.

Nonetheless an important safeguard against humanity's temptation to abuse animals for its own benefit was missing: the idea that God loves animals for their own sake, independent of human needs. During the modern period, from circa 1500 to the middle of the twentieth century, the combination of two central theological claims—that animals were made to serve humanity and that they would not be included in the resurrection—created an attitude among many philosophers and scientists, both Catholic and Protestant, that God was only concerned about the well-being of humanity. That attitude was not so impactful in the Middle Ages; during that era, much of humanity's energy went toward simply surviving all the challenges that nature was throwing at it. But the modern period was a time of great optimism about the growing abilities of human reason to conquer nature through scientific prowess, and in turn, the possibility of fashioning a world more amenable to human flourishing. In short, it was an era distinctively susceptible to human hubris vis-à-vis the world of animals and plants. Those in this period seeking to use and abuse animals for human advancement found that Christian beliefs gave them license to do so.

The Catholic priest and humanist philosopher Marsilio Ficino (1433–99), for example, argued not only that we are to rule over animals but we can do so "cruelly" when it serves our purposes. Humanity is, Ficino stated, the "god without doubt of the animals."[4] In a similar misappropriation of Christian belief, early modern thinkers portrayed their quest to fashion a world hospitable to human flourishing as a new stage in the divinely mandated task of governing creation. Thus the devout Anglican Francis Bacon (1561–1626), sometimes referred to as the father of the scientific method, saw science as a gift from God because it allowed us finally to force nature into our service and make it our "slave" (his word).[5] His fellow Anglican

Robert Boyle (1627–91), another key figure in the development of Western science, asserted that the natural world's *only* purpose was to serve humanity. Any sort of veneration of nature, he maintained, obstructed the noble task God has given to us: establishing our "empire . . . over the inferior creatures of God."[6]

These were not marginal voices. Throughout the modern era, we find scientists and philosophers embracing a convenient view about animals, one they believed grounded in Christian doctrine, in order to argue that humanity was destined by God to rule over the creatures of the earth for its own gain and that science was the tool for effecting that rule.

Perhaps no episode in modern history offers a better example of humanity's theologically inspired hubris toward animals and the natural world than the vivisection debates of the nineteenth century. Experiments on live animals (vivisection) had been almost unknown during the Middle Ages. By the end of the seventeenth century, however, the practice became more common, and in turn opposition to it began to grow, especially as some particularly horrific cases became public. Among the more appalling of these were experiments on live dogs in which their paws were nailed to boards before they were dissected.[7]

The earliest Christian voices against such practices came from Puritan, Quaker, and evangelical (e.g., Methodist) traditions. Eventually, however, significant Anglican voices joined in the criticisms, and in the nineteenth century, a few Catholic critics emerged at odds with mainstream Catholic thought at the time. These critics made impassioned pleas against causing pain to animals and for treating them with Christian kindness and care.

Unfortunately, some Christians, in the pews and pulpits, did not welcome such ideas. One Anglican priest bemoaned that his homily promoting animal welfare disgusted most of his congregation. Likewise, when the Royal Society for the Prevention of Cruelty to Animals (RSPCA) asked permission in 1863 to set up a chapter in Rome, Pope Pius IX denied the request. He explained his rejection by arguing that humanity had no moral duties toward animals. The pope's responses exasperated Frances Power Cobbe, one of the most ardent voices against vivisection in the nineteenth century. Protestants and agnostics, she maintained, were moving forward in battling animal cruelty while Catholics remained closed-hearted before it. She believed that arguments justifying animal abuse on purportedly religious grounds were likely due to "the persuasion of cruel persons that they were God's favourites, and that their victims were either His enemies, or else too humble for His notice."[8]

The pope's statement that humans had no duties toward animals was the standard Catholic position well into the first half of the twentieth century.

We see this in the texts used in Catholic seminaries during the time. The 1935 *Moral and Pastoral Theology*, for example, says: "Animals have no rights," and "we have no duties of justice or charity toward them." Animal suffering in experimental vivisections is ethical because those experiments increase our knowledge of the world.[9] A seminary text on ethics (*Moral Philosophy*) is particularly severe. First published in 1888, it repeats the standard view that animals, because they do not have rational intelligence, cannot have any rights. We have no more obligation to care for them, the book states, than we have to care for plants or stones. The text goes out of its way to relieve the conscience of good Catholics:

> Much more in all that conduces to the sustenance of man may we give pain to brutes [animals], as also in the pursuit of science. Nor are we bound to any anxious care to make this pain as little as may be. Brutes are as *things* in our regard: so far as they are useful to us, they exist for us, not for themselves; and we do right in using them unsparingly for our need and convenience, though not for our wantonness. If then any special case of pain to a brute creature be a fact of considerable value for observation in biological science or the medical art, no reasoned considerations of morality can stand in the way of man making the experiment, yet so that even in the quest of science he be mindful of mercy.[10]

An 1897 book, *Moral Principles and Medical Practice*, was similarly expansive in its permissions, arguing that medical teachers and students can perform experiments on live animals not only for the sake of science but also for training and teaching purposes. Its justification is that "when a brute animal has served man's purpose, it has reached its destiny."[11]

These views do not precisely express the formal teachings of the Church, though their authors often assumed they did. A Catholic teaching only becomes formal (authentic and authoritative) when affirmed in magisterial teaching, either by being part of the unchanging and apostolic Tradition of the Church or by being explicitly presented in an authoritative papal document (e.g., an encyclical or apostolic exhortation) or in the documents of a council. Though it has been the consistent teaching of the Church that humans can use animals, the above arguments support a more extensive, almost unqualified use of animals than what has been formally taught by the Church.

Nonetheless, because Catholic teaching had, until John Paul II, tended to focus much more on humanity's right to use animals than the moral limits of that use, Catholics who found the above arguments wrong and cold-hearted were forced to appeal to biblical themes and to God's direct care for animals. That is, they could not defend their concern for animal well-being against their Catholic opponents by simply appealing to what was commonly understood to be church teachings; arguments based on those teachings tended to favor the pro-experiment position. Rather, they had to look beyond the conventional Catholic views of their day and return instead to the core of Christian belief, the example and teachings of Christ. Thus, it was not uncommon that two contrasting sets of arguments were used by Catholics: one by defenders of animal experiments emphasizing justified use of animals and the other by animal care advocates stressing biblical compassion.

An example of this difference appears in an 1894 exchange of letters published in *The Tablet,* a Catholic weekly based in London. Those defending animal experiments based their arguments on mainstream Catholic views. One respondent reminded readers that animals have no rights and are made for the rational use and benefit of humanity (*The Tablet,* April 7, 1894, 536). Another stated that the idea that a dog could have rights was "embarrassing." A later contributor argued that humans "must be able to inflict pain" on animals for "human convenience and advantage." One writer was particularly blunt: the "sole *raison d'être*" of animals was to serve humanity. Even "wanton disemboweling of beasts alive and without anaesthetics is *in se* an indifferent action" (*The Tablet,* May 19, 1894, 777).

In their counter, animal advocates appealed to the themes and teachings of the Bible. A critic of vivisection cited Proverbs 12:10 ("The just take care of their livestock, but the compassion of the wicked is cruel") to remind readers of God's concern for animals. Another argued that Jesus's command to preach the Gospel to every creature included showing "mercy to animals" (*The Tablet,* April 14, 1894, 577). One contributor argued that experiments on dogs desecrated "one of God's noblest creatures." He described God as "the gentle master" who cares for each fallen sparrow (*The Tablet,* April 21, 1894, 617, referencing Luke 12:6). Another contributor mourned how unfortunate it was "that the Church should seem to lag behind a spontaneous moral movement which is at any rate more in accordance with the Gospel of Christ than its opposite" (*The Tablet,* May 12, 1894, 738).

The Catholic view that animals were created to serve humanity was not the only teaching that came under scrutiny. In the late modern period, at least one animal advocate, Henry S. Salt, speculated that belief in humanity's immortal soul helped rationalize animal abuse. The late nineteenth-century social reformer attributed society's indifference toward animal welfare to the idea that humanity alone has immortality, "thereby furnishing (especially in

Catholic countries) a quibbling justification for acts of cruelty to animals, on the plea that they 'have no souls.'"[12] His critique was off but not entirely wrong. Though there were significant Catholic voices raised against the cruel treatment of animals, they were not prominent among the growing chorus advocating reform, nor were they commonly understood as espousing authentic Catholic teaching. By the end of the nineteenth century, Catholicism was viewed by animal advocates as a recalcitrant force.

CONCLUSION

The Church has no explicit teaching on whether animals will or will not be included in heaven. Aquinas argued not, but Catholics can disagree and still be faithful Catholics. Historically the focus of church teaching in regard to animals has not been on the question of their heavenly future but their God-given role to serve humanity. Nonetheless, until the mid-twentieth century, the consensus among Catholic thinkers was that animals would not be in heaven.

I have suggested that we can recognize the general validity of Aquinas's argument—that resurrecting an animal requires it to have some kind of nonmaterial or spiritual aspect—without accepting its conclusions that only humans can be resurrected. Instead of using a creature's capacity for abstract thinking as a basis for the possibility of resurrection, we could use another criterion: subjectivity or consciousness. I've argued that animals with such capacities have what it takes to be resurrected should God wish to do so. For other creatures (for example, plants and insects), it may be that God will still "save" them but do so by creating replacements of them in heaven.

Aquinas's argument that animals cannot be resurrected due to the particular type of soul they have is not a theological claim grounded in divine revelation. Rather he saw it as the fruit of natural human reason, an insight gained by observing both humans and animals and drawing conclusions about the type of soul that each creature had.

The Church's teaching on animals was not pressed to develop beyond a few basic commitments until it was faced with the controversies about animal cruelty that erupted during the modern period, especially in the nineteenth century. Some Catholic thinkers began to approach animals in a more explicitly Christian framework during the period. In their advocacy for animals, they appealed not only to human reason but also to distinctively Christian ideals and Gospel values. Their views, however, generally remained at the margins of Catholic thought until the Second Vatican Council (Vatican II).

NOTES

1. Emily Anthes, "How Science Went to the Dogs (and Cats)," *New York Times*, June 30, 2024.
2. Among other places, Aquinas develops his argument in I.75 of his *Summa Theologiae*. For this and all other texts from Aquinas's *Summa Theologiae*, I will use the following translation from the English Dominican Fathers (London: Burns, Oates & Washbourne, 1932). The translation is available online at New Advent, https://www.newadvent.org/summa/. For a more complete and technical overview of Aquinas's views, see Linda Farmer, "Straining the Limits of Philosophy: Aquinas on the Immortality of the Human Soul," *Faith and Philosophy: Journal of the Society of Christian Philosophers*, 20, no. 2 (2003): 208–17.
3. Aquinas, *Summa Theologiae*, III.Supplement.91.1 c. and 92.1 c.
4. Charles E. Trinkhaus, *In Our Image and Likeness: Humanity and Divinity in Italian Humanist Thought*, vol. 2 (Notre Dame, IN: University of Notre Dame Press, 1970), 484.
5. Benjamin Farrington, *The Philosophy of Francis Bacon: An Essay on Its Development from 1603 to 1609* (Liverpool: Liverpool University Press, 1964), 62.
6. Robert Boyle, *A Free Enquiry into the Vulgarly Received Notion of Nature* (London: Early English Books, 1686), 18–19.
7. Leonora Rosenfield, *From Beast-Machine to Man-Machine: Animal Soul in French Letters from Descartes to La Mettrie* (New York: Octagon Books, 1968), 54.
8. Frances Power Cobbe, "The Ethics of Zoophily," *Contemporary Review*, 68 (October 1895), 506.
9. Henry Davis, *Moral and Pastoral Theology*, 2nd ed., vol. 2 (London: Sheed & Ward, 1935), 258.
10. Joseph Rickaby, *Moral Philosophy: Or, Ethics and Natural Law*, 2nd ed. (London: Longmans, Green; Internet Archive, 1888), 250 (emphasis in original).
11. Charles Coppens, *Moral Principles and Medical Practice, the Basis of Medical Jurisprudence* (New York: Benziger Brothers; Internet Archive, 1897), 42.
12. Henry Stephens Salt, *Animals' Rights Considered in Relation to Social Progress* (New York: Macmillan; Internet Archive, 1894), 8. Technically, animals do have souls in Aquinas's thought but not immortal ones.

FURTHER READING

Most of the sources for this chapter's discussions can be found in chapter 1 of *All God's Animals: A Catholic Theological Framework for Animal Ethics*. Washington, DC: Georgetown University Press, 2019, 8–55.

Church Documents

Most Catholic Church documents are available on the Vatican website, www.vatican.va.
The Vatican's website has a portal for each pope where their writings, homilies, addresses, and other public statements can be found: https://www.vatican.va/holy_father/index.htm.

The *Catechism of the Catholic Church* is available here: https://www.vatican.va/archive/ENG0015/_INDEX.HTM.
Documents published by the Vatican's International Theological Commission are listed here: https://www.vatican.va/roman_curia/congregations/cfaith/cti_documents/rc_cti_index-doc-pubbl_en.html.

Thomas Aquinas and Souls

Thompson, Christopher J. Thompson. *The Joyful Mystery: Field Notes toward a Green Thomism*. Steubenville, OH: Emmaus Road Publishing, 2017.
Murphy, Nancey C. *Bodies and Souls, or Spirited Bodies?* Cambridge: Cambridge University Press, 2006.
An online translation of Thomas Aquinas's *Summa Theologiae* is provided on the New Advent website: https://www.newadvent.org/summa/.
For a helpful overview of biblical portrayals of the soul, see Ray S. Anderson, "On Being Human: The Spiritual Saga of a Creaturely Soul." In *Whatever Happened to the Soul? Scientific and Theological Portraits of Human Nature*. Edited by Warren S. Brown, Nancey C. Murphy, and H. Newton Malony, 175–94. Minneapolis: Fortress Press, 1998.

The History of Treatment of Animals

Carson, Gerald. *Men, Beasts, and Gods: A History of Cruelty and Kindness to Animals*. New York: Charles Scribner's Sons, 1970.
Thomas, Keith. *Man and the Natural Word: Changing Attitudes in England 1500–1800*. New York: Oxford University Press, 1983.
Turner, E. S. *All Heaven in a Rage*. New York: St. Martin's Press, 1965.

Companion Animals (Pets)

Grimm, David. *Citizen Canine: Our Evolving Relationship with Cats and Dogs*. Philadelphia: Perseus Books, 2014.

CHAPTER 2

Context for Change

In 1967, as the looming perils of environmental degradation were beginning to seep into the Western consciousness, Lynn White Jr., an American historian and active Presbyterian, penned an explosive article, "The Historical Roots of Our Ecologic Crisis."[1] In the short, five-page essay, White argued that Western science and technology have been infected by a "Christian arrogance toward nature." The ecological crisis, he believed, will only continue to worsen until science and technology are purged of this arrogance and Christians reject the "axiom that nature has no reason for existence save to serve man."

The article was instrumental in raising the environment as a legitimate topic of Christian theological discourse. In the wake of the contentious discussions it fostered, the Christian community came to recognize a pressing need to become involved in the issue, marshalling its distinctive resources in order to address a crisis that, according to the essay, it had been complicit in creating. The article has its flaws, but it continues to fuel debates, both within and without Christianity, and has become a foundational document for Christian environmental theology.

Discussions like these form the context in which the Church does its thinking about animals and the natural world, learning from the wisdom of others but interpreting their claims in light of the Church's religious commitments. Galvanized by contemporary needs, Catholicism has, over the last half-century or so, rethought its attitudes toward the nonhuman world, the language it uses to describe that world, and its understanding of our responsibilities for it. In doing so, the Church shows its fidelity to the task identified by Vatican II, the "duty of scrutinizing the signs of the times and of interpreting them in the light of the Gospel" (*Gaudium et Spes*, §4). The Gospel message is perennial, but the Church knows that its understanding of that message will develop in accord with new insights and in response to the needs and dramas of our social existence.

A number of factors have shaped the contemporary context in which the Church does its thinking about the natural world, but I'll note three here: the already-mentioned environmental crisis, animal theodicy, and contemporary science on animals. Of the three, the first has had an outsized importance, but the other two are perhaps weightier in the challenge that they raise regarding two fundamental Christian commitments: God's goodness and the uniqueness of the human person vis-à-vis all other creatures.

Finally, I will describe a fourth factor that has given the Church the theological resources for responding to these developments: a minority tradition, already present in Catholicism, for which the good news of Jesus Christ is also good news for animals.

THE ENVIRONMENTAL CRISIS

Most of us are well aware of the basics of our environmental crisis; it forms part of an ominous background fueling contemporary anxieties. At this point, we have entered a second and graver phase of the crisis. The first phase, fully underway in the 1970s, entailed localized damage: waterways polluted by toxic runoff, hazardous urban air quality, soil contamination at specific locations, and pesticide harms to local wildlife. In contrast to the earlier phase, we are now confronting a threat to the entire global ecosystem and the possibility of its collapse. The facts are disturbing. Among those identified by a report of the United Nations Environment Programme are the following:

> One million of the world's estimated 8 million species of plants and animals are threatened with extinction. . . . Close to 90% of the world's marine fish stocks are fully exploited, overexploited or depleted. . . . Around 3.2 billion people, or 40 percent of the global population, are adversely affected by land degradation. . . . 100–300 million people are at increased risk of floods and hurricanes because of coastal habitat loss.[2]

In response to growing environmental concerns, exhortations for environmental care began to appear in magisterial documents starting with Pope Paul VI's *Octogesima Adveniens* (1971) and his "Message to the Stockholm

Conference on the Human Environment" (1972). Subsequent popes—John Paul II, Benedict XVI, and Francis—have underscored with ever greater forcefulness the preciousness of creation and have exhorted the global community to protect it against environmental abuse.

The Church's endeavor since Vatican II to foster care for creation has led it to mine its own distinctive resources—for example, appealing to the idea that nature is a wondrous gift from God that expresses his glory and gives him praise. Such appeals also serve to underscore a theological issue at stake in the environmental crisis: God cares about creation, and thus so must we. Creation is a "gift" that is "to become *God's* garden" (Benedict, "Homily: Vigil of Pentecost," June 6, 2006, emphasis added). Though an emphasis on God's love for creation does not in itself argue that God wills to save nonhuman creatures, it is an apt conclusion, and since Vatican II, the Church has progressed toward embracing it.

ANIMAL THEODICY AND EVOLUTION

In the early eighteenth century, the German philosopher Gottfried Leibniz coined the term "theodicy" to refer to the endeavor by Christian thinkers to defend God's goodness in the face of human suffering. The issue was not a new one for Christianity, but challenges to God's goodness and the perceived legitimacy of those challenges grew during the modern period. Tragic historical events—like the Lisbon earthquake on All Saints Day in 1755, which killed upward of 40,000 people out of a total population of 200,000 and leveled most of its buildings, including churches—made defending God's goodness more urgent.

As debates about animal cruelty heated up during the modern period, Christian defenders were called upon to expand the scope of their theodicies and include the issue of animal suffering: How could a good and loving God allow animals, creatures incapable of sin, to suffer? Amplifying the challenge was an increasing recognition within the scientific community that animals and humans were more physiologically similar than earlier believed. This not only raised the possibility that animals could suffer with the depth experienced by humans but also placed into question the radical discontinuity that had long been assumed to exist between humans and all other creatures. If animals and humans shared anatomical features, one might be tempted to believe they also shared spiritual ones (e.g., an immortal soul).

The Catholic philosopher René Descartes (d. 1650) developed a theory that solved both problems, the suffering of animals and their supposed similarity to humanity. Descartes attributed to the soul all that is commonly associated with subjective experience (thought, sensation, and feeling) and then excluded those same attributes from animals. Humans had souls; animals did not. Because animals were soulless, they were also devoid of consciousness and passion; they were basically machines, if complicated ones. Lacking sentience, animals could not experience painful feelings.

Not only did this preserve the human/animal distinction, it had the added benefit of alleviating any distress one might feel over the suffering of animals. Descartes was aware of this implication and endorsed it. The soul/body distinction is, he wrote, "indulgent to human beings . . . since it absolves them from the suspicion of crime when they eat or kill animals."[3] The French priest Nicholas Malebranche and the Catholic philosopher Antoine Arnauld, followers of Descartes, were said to demonstrate their confidence in this view by beating dogs in front of skeptics and announcing to the dismayed spectators that the dogs could feel no pain.[4] The tortured animals, they claimed, only *appeared* to have feelings.

Some Catholic thinkers appealed to theodicy in order to deny, against everyday experience and commonplace assumptions, that animals genuinely suffer. Animals, whether in the lab or in their natural habitats, do not have the capacity to suffer, they claimed, because if they *were* able to suffer, it would undermine Christian belief in God's goodness. Since animals are not moral beings—they cannot freely choose and so cannot sin—they do not deserve to suffer. Therefore, God, since he is good, cannot permit such a thing to happen. The Catholic priest Nicholas Poisson, for example, argued in 1670 that it would violate God's justice to create an animal who could experience pain that it did nothing to deserve. Cardinal Melchoir de Polignac (d. 1742) maintained that if innocent animals really suffered, it would threaten not only God's justice but our own. We would be daily guilty of cruelty.[5]

Regardless of how dubious they might have found Descartes's understanding of animals, Christian philosophers recognized that the Cartesian appeal to theodicy highlighted a significant vulnerability in Christian belief. If animals could genuinely and gravely suffer, how could Christians defend the goodness of God? The only path forward for Catholics would be to modify basic beliefs—for example, to maintain that God *also* saves animals, thereby redeeming their earthly suffering. Instead Catholic thinkers defended traditional views by vainly trying to deny the facts or fabricate new ones.

Thus, in another argument straining credibility, the French philosopher David Boullier maintained in 1728 that although animals have souls, their suffering would impugn divine justice only if the suffering was so grave that it would be better if they had never existed, a condition that God prevents from occurring. Also embracing a form of divine micromanaging, Jean-Pierre de Crousaz claimed in 1773 that animals did not suffer greatly because God made sure that any suffering endured by the animals was outweighed by their pleasures. In the most outrageous explanation, Fr. Guillaume-Hyacinthe Bougeant mused in 1739, perhaps in jest, that God punished demons by forcing them to animate the bodies of animals. The demon supplied the consciousness, while the animal's body provided everything else. Animals had souls but not their own. Any suffering was experienced only by the demon who, as Bougeant noted, deserved it.

Eventually these arguments were dismissed as the tide of common sense rose against them. That these contorted attempts to preserve God's goodness in light of animal suffering were ultimately unsuccessful is itself an argument in favor of animals in heaven: The failure of the arguments underscores the difficulty in preserving belief in God's goodness without the promise of a future life for those suffering in the present.

The challenge raised by animal suffering still haunts theology today, and contemporary reports of the natural world's brutality have made addressing it more difficult. The problem confronting Catholics since the mid-twentieth century, as the theory of evolution became theologically acceptable, is not only that individual animals suffer gravely, problematic as that is. Theologians must also explain how a good and loving God chose evolution, with all its violence, as the means for creating the world.

The natural world is not just cruel; it can be almost diabolical in that the well-being of some animals directly depends on the brutal death of others. Female pelicans lay two eggs. The chicks fight among themselves (with the mother's support) until one of them is killed, directly or by being rejected from the nest. The giant water bug injects venomous digestive saliva into its prey so that it can suck the internal organs out for its nourishment. Charles Darwin was famously disturbed by the practice of wasps inserting their eggs inside the living bodies of white caterpillars (upon hatching, the larvae eat their way out of the caterpillar). Such brutality, so at odds with romanticized depictions of the natural world, led Darwin to decry "the clumsy wasteful, blundering, low, and horribly cruel works of nature!"[6] It is difficult to reconcile these and other examples of animal suffering with the loving Creator revealed in Jesus Christ.

Evolutionary theory further complicates the endeavor to defend God's goodness by challenging a fundamental teaching that has been critical to that defense: the absolute distinction between humans and nonhumans.

The distinction helps explain and justify the difference in the loving care that God gives to each group (i.e., eternal salvation for one group and eternal death for the other). With evolution, the absoluteness of the distinction becomes less plausible, at least on a biological level, given that we not only share a common evolutionary history with other animals but also have a significantly overlapping DNA profile with many of them (98% overlap with chimpanzees, 84% with dogs, and 67% with mice). Further thwarting the attempt to sharply separate humans from all nonhumans is scientific evidence suggesting that Neanderthals and humans overlapped geographically for 30,000 years or more, during which time they interbred.

The threat to a neat human/nonhuman binary is particularly acute when considered historically, in terms of those times when the differences between early humans and some species of nonhuman animals were smaller and less dramatic. To put a fine point on the issue, we can consider this evolutionary scenario: At the first appearance of the human person, some animal mother who, according to traditional teaching, did *not* have an immortal soul gave birth to a child who did. Her child was destined to eternal life with God; she was not. The utter difference between the care that God has for human creatures and the lack of such care for protohuman ones is hard to reconcile with God's goodness. If we were, however, to try and address the problem by arguing that God's salvific concern *also* extends to protohumans, then we have to wonder, why stop there? Perhaps God's salvation includes other nonhumans—creatures like dolphins, ducks, and dingoes.

The possibility of defending God's goodness in the face of these challenges by arguing that God *also* saves animals was not seen as a viable option by Catholic thinkers up through the modern period, but that is changing. Though the hope that animals will ultimately be saved does not, by itself, explain why God allows their suffering, it does provide an important, if partial, step in preserving the fundamental goodness of the world God created. With the gift of salvation, the pain and grief of God's creatures in the present age, both human and nonhuman, will not be the last chapter in any of their stories.

SCIENCE AND ANIMALS

Scientific discoveries about animals suggest that the cognitive and social capabilities of some are closer to humans than previously recognized. I focus here on those animals (terrestrial and aquatic) with significant cognitive capacities. I do so to underscore the significance of the problem: The *functional* differences between humans and higher animals like the bonobos, though still substantial to my mind, are not *by themselves* enough to sustain the neat theological and ethical divisions assumed in Catholic thought. Dividing up earthly creatures into just two categories, the human and the nonhuman, has the effect of placing an animal like Koko, the linguistically talented gorilla, in the same theological category as fleas. Such a crude grouping might have seemed sensible in an earlier era; reigning assumptions about the lack of any theologically significant differences in capacities among nonhuman animals excluded more nuanced considerations. We now recognize that the simple, twofold division is strained, at least from what we can observe empirically. Not only are we all, humans and nonhumans, creatures of the same God but also descendants of the same creaturely ancestors, and this shared ancestry has given nonhuman animals a range of capabilities, some of which approach those of humanity.

Scientific assumptions that dominated well into the middle of the twentieth century tended to view animals within a stimulus–response framework: Scientists explained animal behavior in terms of seeking rewards and avoiding pain. In contrast, contemporary ethologists (scientists studying animal behavior and psychology) recognize that animal behavior is often guided by a cognitively rich and complex internal life. Such discoveries would have once been dismissed as anthropomorphic projections, false attributions of features that belong only to humans. No longer.

Recent decades have seen an explosion of evidence of these advanced capabilities, including ones that had been used to defend human uniqueness—foresight, reasoning, memory, language, self-awareness, and capacity for friendship. For example, orangutans are known escape artists; they can stealthily and with strategizing foresight dismantle their cages across several weeks, deliberately hiding their escape plans from their keepers.[7] A number of chimpanzees and orangutans have succeeded in an intelligence test that only 58% of eight-year-olds are able to pass.[8] Sometimes an aspect of animal intelligence is superior not only to that of young children but also to that of adults: One study showed young chimpanzees have a better ability to memorize a series of numbers than the typical human adult.[9]

Tool use had been viewed not only as a sign of intelligence but also as a uniquely human ability. Again upending traditional views, a number of tool-using animals have been discovered in recent decades, demonstrating the thoughtful ingenuity of our fellow animal creatures. Chimpanzees hunting for honey in Gabon, for example, have developed an elaborate tool kit made up of five pieces that are used sequentially to gather honey (thus evidencing foresight, planning, and a sense of cause and effect).[10] Primates are not the only ones who use tools. Bottlenose dolphins carefully choose sponges that fit on their noses. They then wield these sponges to gently shift the sand on the ocean floor and flush out hidden fish burrowed below the surface, a practice that is not instinctive but must be taught by mothers in each generation.[11] Tool-users can also be found among avians. One study showed New Caledonian crows inventing tools in order to retrieve food.[12]

Only in the latter part of the twentieth century did scientists begin serious investigations into the interior life of animals (e.g., their emotional life and ability to suffer). The issue is difficult to study, not only because scientists have no direct experience of animal consciousness but also because, as I've noted, they have not identified a physiological explanation for human consciousness.

The issues are complex, but for the sake of our discussion, it suffices to note that consciousness occurs within the animal world across a multifaceted spectrum, incorporating one or more qualities like a basic capacity to experience stimuli as painful and pleasurable, a basic subjective awareness of experience, and a self-awareness by which the animal reflects on itself. Demonstrating a growing consensus regarding the richness of the interior life of animals, an international group of prominent scientists declared in 2012 that "the weight of evidence indicates that humans are not unique in possessing the neurological substrates that generate consciousness."[13]

To ascertain whether an animal is self-aware, scientists have appealed to the mirror test. The basis of the test is that animals with self-awareness will react differently upon seeing their reflected images in a mirror compared to those who are not self-aware—the former will examine their bodies, and the latter will ignore the reflection or treat it as another animal. The test sometimes involves the administration of a mark on the animal's body at a location outside its visual range. Self-aware animals know to use the mirror to look at the mark. Animals who have passed the test represent species as diverse as Asian elephants, nonhuman members of the great ape family (bonobos, chimpanzees, orangutans, and gorillas), bottlenose dolphins, orca whales, and Eurasian magpies.

One of the more uplifting discoveries made by scientists is the varied and highly developed sociality found among animals. Though the idea of animal friendship might be dismissed as a romantic anthropomorphism (in some cases deservedly so), scientists recognize that there is some truth underlying the heartwarming accounts of animal friendships appearing in social media. Social interactions within the animal world include friendships not only between individuals of the same species (conspecifics) but also between animals of different species. Among the friendships within species that have been studied are female friendships (chimpanzees, horses, whales), male friendships (spider monkeys, horses, lions, penguins), and elderly companions (baboons, elephants, buffaloes). The occasional appearance of cross-species friendships (e.g., a badger and a coyote, a dog and an elephant, a wolf and two goats) suggest that friendships are critically important for some species, and if animals are not able to be friends with their conspecifics, they will try to form friendships with members of other species.[14]

Famous in their development and complexity are the social networks of elephants. Guided by their matriarch, elephants have fairly clear social roles within the herd and learn how to work with their herd-mates in order to achieve desired ends—for example, assisting disabled members and protecting those who are wounded in assaults. Elephants regularly establish special bonds with other members of their herd, especially females, whose long-term friendships can last sixty years or more. The species has become a social media sensation as its grieving rituals have come to light. These rituals include spending hours at the location of a deceased relative days after her death. The bonds of affection and the grief that ensues upon the death of a herd-mate are intense for elephants—akin, it would seem, to those of human families. One researcher played a recording of a deceased elephant. "The family went wild calling, looking all around. The dead elephant's daughter called for days afterward."[15]

Although the Christian tradition has seen reason as the distinguishing mark of humanity, a more appropriate candidate might be moral choice, given the centrality of love to Christianity. The evidence as to whether animals have the capacity to make moral decisions is mixed. Studies show that animals have something like moral passions and drives (an evolutionary development that some argue arose to help animals negotiate their social environments). The question that such studies raise, however, is whether or to what degree these moral passions allow animals to make something like a genuine moral choice—that is, one that involves reasoned reflection undertaken by the animal before it chooses how to act. Though there is ample evidence that animals act in ways that can be described in moral terms, for now it seems that humans are distinct in regard to moral deliberations. Not only do we experience moral desires, we can also reflect on them and assess the merits of acting on them, ultimately asking whether a considered course of action is morally good (i.e., good in itself, not just good for us) before making a decision.

The above sample of findings by scientists challenges the neatly bounded difference between humans and nonhumans that theological discussions have long assumed. We are, nonetheless, still able to affirm the functional distinctiveness of humanity (e.g., in our highly developed capacities for reflexive moral agency and theoretical reasoning), but the chasm between humanity and at least some animals in regard to capabilities appears less wide than had been assumed. And if the *functional* chasm separating the abilities of humans from those of nonhumans is not so great, then perhaps the *salvific* chasm—the gap between God's salvific response to humans and his response to nonhumans—is not so great either.

Though it's doubtful that scientific findings on animals have had any *direct* influence on the recent shift in church teaching on animals, these findings do show that the natural world is far more interesting, complex, and developed than previously realized, and this understanding has filtered down to become part of our culture's intellectual background. When it comes to animals, contemporary culture has come to anticipate amazement, to expect the unexpected.

THE MINORITY TRADITION

The almost exclusively anthropocentric approach to animals described in chapter 1 had been dominant until the eve of the Second Vatican Council. However, this approach represented only one strand in the Catholic tradition, and in recent decades, as threats to the natural world have grown, the Church has increasingly appealed to an alternative strand, what I'll call the minority tradition.[16] In its recovery of this tradition, the Church has engaged in a practice common during the years leading up to Vatican II: the creative retrieval of earlier Christian sources to update contemporary church theology.

In contrast to modern views, a number of early Christian thinkers believed that all creation would be liberated by Christ. For example, one of the Church's earliest theologians, St. Irenaeus of Lyons (d. 202), argued that Christ's labor encompassed all creation based on the idea, found in the opening verses of Colossians and Ephesians, that Christ is the end point of all creation. We will return to these passages in the next chapter, but their core point is that, from the beginning of creation, God had a plan to bring all creation to its fulfillment under the aegis of Christ, so that all things would be "summed up" in him. Irenaeus was not alone in this approach. St. Maximus the Confessor (d. 662) held that God's goal in creating the cosmos was to bring all creatures into harmony with one another and draw them together as one with Christ; the result would be a cosmic symphony of all creatures praising God.

St. John Chrysostom (d. 407) used a different set of arguments but arrived at the same conclusion: Nonhuman creatures will be saved. He tied the fate of nonhuman creatures to humanity's redemption and concluded that all creation will share in humanity's final transformation. In a homily on chapter 8 of Romans, Chrysostom made two arguments in support of the claim. First, he argued that just as nonhuman creation suffered disease and death due to human sin, so also creation will, like the human body, become free of those punishments when God redeems humanity. Second, he appealed to the example of a nurse caring for a child who is destined to become king. When the child is elevated to the throne, the nurse will also be elevated and thus will share in the king's joys and blessings. Similarly, animals, which were created to serve humanity, will be lifted up when God transforms humanity so that humanity's joys will overflow to include all creatures.

Other voices supporting an animal-inclusive salvation include St. Ephrem the Syrian (d. 373)—who states that in the next age God will grant "paschal joy" to all animals—and St. Athanasius of Alexandria (d. 373)—who argues that animals, through their common bond with humanity, will share in humanity's divinization.

Though these voices were important and influential in the first centuries, their views on animals were generally sidelined during the medieval and modern periods in the West. Given their stature, that's surprising. All of them have been declared "Doctors of the Church," either formally or, in the case of Maximus, informally by Pope Benedict. They are among the thirty-seven saints (thirty-eight if we include Maximus) whose theologies are considered particularly trustworthy guides by the Church (out of the over 10,000 individuals declared saints by the Catholic Church).

Rather than relying on the more traditional—and, one suspects, ultimately less demanding—standard of "reasonableness," this minority tradition embraced Gospel ideals to guide how we treat animals. We've already seen this emphasis in the last chapter, where some Catholics in the modern period made their case for animal care by appealing to Gospel values and the teachings of Jesus. We also find witnesses to these ideals in the lives of the saints. Among these practitioners of animal kindness, St. Francis of Assisi is the most well-known, but he is not alone. The *Acta Sanctorum* (a collection detailing the lives of Catholic saints) is filled with other saintly examples.[17] In a few cases, these saints even preached the Gospel to animals. St. Anthony of Padua (d. 1231), for example, told fish that they owed the "Creator a vast debt of gratitude," since, among other things, God left them "unmolested" by the waters of the flood, and they were given the privilege of "furnishing the tribute money for the Word Incarnate" (i.e., the Roman tax described in Matthew 17:24–27).[18]

Some of these accounts are probably partly or entirely fictional, but their historical accuracy is not what interests me. Rather the circulation of so many of these stories shows the great admiration elicited by such stories of animal care in Catholic piety across the centuries.

In words and teachings, two nineteenth-century cardinals, St. John Henry Newman and Henry Edward Manning, also promoted a standard of Christlike care for animals. In a homily, Newman compares the suffering of Christ on the cross to that of animals abused domestically and those used for experiments. He likens individuals guilty of such abuse to the evildoers who crucified Christ and condemns them as barbarous and cold-blooded. Newman assumes that Christian obligations to animals go beyond just a duty to avoid inflicting excessive suffering. He composed a novena to St. Philip Neri, the one other saint besides Francis of Assisi commended by the *Catechism of the Catholic Church* as a model for animal care. In it Newman seeks the grace of charity toward all of God's creatures: "Philip, my glorious Advocate, teach me to look at all I see around me after thy pattern as creatures of God. Let me never forget that the same God who made me, made the whole world, and all men and animals that are in it. Gain me the grace to love all God's works for God's sake."

Though Newman supported legislation giving protection to animals, the Catholic voice most associated with animal advocacy at the time was that of Cardinal Manning (1808–1892). The cardinal regularly gave speeches in support of stricter rules for experiments on animals and argued that vivisection was not how God wanted us to make advances in medicine. Manning bristled at Pius IX's rejection of the RSPCA in 1863. He accepted the traditional view that humans do not owe any duties *directly* toward animals but argued that since they are God's creatures, not ours, we have a duty to God to treat them mercifully. Apparently Manning also spoke privately to Pius IX's successor, Leo XIII, after his election as pope (1878) and raised concerns about experiments on animals. Though papal teaching did not undergo any substantial change, subsequent popes did embrace the cause of animal protection. Leo's successor, Pius X (r. 1903–1914), sent his blessing on "all who protect from abuse and cruelty the dumb servants given to us by God" (*The Tablet*, July 28, 1906), and Benedict XV (r. 1914–1922) personally donated a thousand lire to Rome's Society for the Protection of Animals (*The Tablet*, September 6, 1919).

The argument that we should treat animals with Christlike care does not, of course, translate into proof that animals will join us in the age to come. However, if we accept the view that Christ's love is also directed toward animals, the idea that he will also include them in his salvific gift seems an appropriate inference. At least one seminary text of the modern era drew that connection—*Foundations of Morality: God, Man, Lower Creatures* (1936) by the German priest and theologian Ludwig Ruland.[19]

The basic starting points of Ruland's approach are consistent with prevalent views at the time: An essential difference exists between human persons and animals, animals can be used for medical experiments, and animals do not have immortal souls or rational abilities. However, Ruland makes a claim that is unexpected, given his historical context. He says that despite humanity's "great progress" in many other moral matters, we have failed to progress in our treatment of animals. We have a "wrong attitude toward the animal world" due to a "primitively anthropomorphic view of nature, coupled with the mistaken idea that we know virtually everything about animal life" (Ruland, p. 366). He expects our moral norms for animals will continue to develop so that they ever more closely come to reflect Christlike care. "The beautiful harmony" displayed "between the saints and the animals" is the standard we should progress toward in our treatment of animals (Ruland, p. 371).

He makes the additional claim, also atypical for the time, that the present circumstance of animals is not their final state. Using an argument similar to Chrysostom's, he states, "As the curse of sin affects the whole creation, so all creatures are to experience the blessing of redemption" (Ruland, p. 369). He goes on to say that because "all creation has been redeemed in Christ," our treatment of animals must reflect the "likeness of God's rule" (Ruland, p. 370). Thus as Christians progress in the love of God, they will also increasingly attend to the groaning of God's creatures and "see in suffering animals the plea for mercy and love in the name of God" (Ruland, p. 373). Catholic advocates for animals have been making similar claims, both theological and ethical, in recent decades. That Ruland made them almost a century ago is prophetic.

Thus while the dominant Catholic tradition has emphasized the role of animals as servants of humanity to be reasonably used and offered them no hope of life after death, a different and more animal-friendly tradition in Catholicism developed alongside the dominant one. This minority tradition appealed to a specifically Christlike attitude to determine how God wants us to treat animals. Many of the voices that composed this minority tradition believed that Christ's salvific work extended to the entire cosmos, not just to human persons. In the second half of the twentieth century, the Church began to retrieve insights from this minority tradition and move them to the center of its theological discussions.

CONCLUSION

It is unimaginable that any contemporary pope would follow Pius IX's example and reject an animal advocacy group based on the claim that we have no moral duties to animals. Something has changed since the first half of the twentieth century. The Church's turn toward a more creation- and animal-friendly interpretation of God's salvific labor is not revolutionary, but the shift is, nonetheless, real and significant. Fortunately for the Church, it was an easy shift to make: The resources for the change were already available in a minority tradition that formed part of Catholicism's rich heritage.

The looming climate crisis has likely been a key factor in the Church's increasingly emphatic reminders of God's concern for creation and our responsibility to it; however, two other factors are significant, if less directly impactful. First, since the modern period, the Church has struggled to respond persuasively to the challenge of theodicy, defending divine justice in a world of innocent suffering, both human and nonhuman. The growing acceptance of evolutionary theory has additionally required us to make sense of how a good and loving God could create a world through a process so cruel in its mechanisms. Second, we live at a time when science is progressively revealing to us the complex beauty and stunning capabilities of the natural world; the traditional placement of all nonhuman animals in the same category of irrational creatures has become inadequate in the face of both the diversity of animal forms and the growing scientific insights about them and the biosystems of our world.

One other factor was critical as an initial catalyst for the Church's shift: the Second Vatican Council and its embrace of a "cosmic eschatology"—the belief that God's salvific labor has a cosmic scope. Providing support for that teaching were the voices noted previously, early church thinkers who maintained that all the creatures of the earth will share in God's salvation. Vatican II embraced this theology of the end times (eschatology) but was vague on the specifics of it, leaving it to the post-conciliar Church to fill in the details, a task undertaken by recent popes. In chapter 4, we will examine Vatican II and the influence that its eschatology had on the teachings of popes John Paul II, Benedict XVI, and Francis.

NOTES

1. Lynn White Jr., "The Historical Roots of Our Ecologic Crisis," *Science* 155, no. 3767 (1967): 1203–7.
2. United Nations: Environment Programme, "Facts about the Nature Crisis," https://www.unep.org/facts-about-nature-crisis.

3. René Descartes, *The Philosophical Writings of Descartes: The Correspondence*, vol. 3, trans. John Cottingham et al. (Cambridge: Cambridge University Press, 1991), 366.
4. Ulrich Tröhler and Andreas-Holger Maehle, "Animal Experimentation from Antiquity to the End of the Eighteenth Century: Attitudes and Arguments," in *Vivisection in Historical Perspective*, ed. Nicolaas A. Rupke (New York: Croom Helm, 1987), 26–27.
5. For many of the historical details of this paragraph and the next two, I'm indebted to Lloyd Strickland, "God's Creatures? Divine Nature and the Status of Animals in the Early Modern Beast-Machine Controversy," *International Journal of Philosophy and Theology* 74, no. 4 (December 2013): 291–309.
6. Charles Darwin, "Letter to J.D. Hooker," *More Letters of Charles Darwin: A Record of His Work in a Series of Hitherto Unpublished Letters*, ed. Francis Darwin and A. C. Seward, vol. 1 (London: Hazel, Watson, and Viny, 1903), 94.
7. Frans de Waal, *Are We Smart Enough to Know How Smart Animals Are?* (New York: W. W. Norton, 2016), 81.
8. De Waal, 91–92. In the "floating peanut task," a peanut is placed at the bottom of a tube. The animals (or eight-year-old children) must figure out that they need to add water to the tube in order to reach the peanut.
9. Sana Inoue and Tetsuro Matsuzawa, "Working Memory of Numerals in Chimpanzees," *Current Biology* 17, no. 23 (December 2007).
10. De Waal, 79.
11. Janet Mann et al., "Social Networks Reveal Cultural Behaviour in Tool-Using Dolphins," *Nature Communications* 3 (December 2012).
12. A. M. P. von Bayern et al., "Compound Tool Construction by New Caledonian Crows," *Scientific Reports* 8, 15676 (2018).
13. Philip Low, "The Cambridge Declaration on Consciousness," The Francis Crick Memorial Conference, Churchill College, Cambridge University, July 7, 2012, 1–2.
14. See Anne Dagg, *Animal Friendships* (New York: Cambridge University Press, 2011).
15. Carl Safina, *Beyond Words: What Animals Think and Feel* (New York: Picador, 2016), 67.
16. For a developed account of the tensions in the Christian tradition regarding the environment, see Paul H. Santmire, *The Travail of Nature: The Ambiguous Ecological Promise of Christian Theology* (Minneapolis, MN: Augsburg Fortress, 1991).
17. The *Acta Sanctorum* is a sixty-eight-volume encyclopedia of the lives of Catholic saints published between 1643 and 1940. An English translation of some of the entries can be found in *The Church and Kindness to Animals* (London: Burns & Oates, 1906), whose author is anonymous.
18. *Church and Kindness*, 50.
19. Ludwig Ruland, *Foundation of Morality: God, Man, Lower Creatures*, trans. Tarcisius Anthony Rattler and Newton Wayland Thompson (Saint Louis: B. Herder, 1936).

FURTHER READING

More details about this chapter's discussions can be found in *All God's Animals: A Catholic Theological Framework for Animal Ethics*. Washington, DC: Georgetown University Press, 2019, 38–41, 68–76, and 99–106.

Church Documents

The most significant Catholic Church documents are available on the Vatican website, www.vatican.va.

The Vatican's website has a portal for each pope where their writings, homilies, audiences, and public statements can be found: https://www.vatican.va/holy_father/index.htm.

Theology, Spirituality, and Animals

The Church and Kindness to Animals. London: Burns & Oates, 1906.

Camosy, Charles. *For Love of Animals: Christian Ethics, Consistent Action*. Cincinnati, OH: Franciscan Media, 2013.

Hobgood-Oster, Laura. *The Friends We Keep: Unleashing Christianity's Compassion for Animals*. Waco, TX: Baylor University Press, 2010.

Jones, Deborah. *The School of Compassion: A Roman Catholic Theology of Animals*. Leominster, England: Gracewing Publishing, 2009.

Schaefer, Jame. *Theological Foundations for Environmental Ethics: Reconstructing Patristic and Medieval Concepts*. Washington, DC: Georgetown University Press, 2009.

Theodicy and Animal Suffering

Hughes, Gerard J. *Is God to Blame? The Problem of Evil Revisted*. Dublin: Veritas, 2007.

Southgate, Christopher. *The Groaning of Creation: God, Evolution, and the Problem of Evil*. Louisville: Westminster John Knox Press, 2008.

Theology, Evolution, and Animals

Edwards, Denis. *The God of Evolution: A Trinitarian Theology*. New York: Paulist Press, 1999.

Haught, John. *God after Darwin: A Theology of Evolution*. London: Routledge, 2007.

Johnson, Elizabeth A. *Ask the Beasts: Darwin and the God of Love*. New York: Bloomsbury, 2015.

Polkinghorne, John C. *Exploring Reality: The Intertwining of Science and Religion*. New Haven, CT: Yale University Press, 2005.

Contemporary Science and Animals

Bekoff, Mark. *Why Dogs Hump and Bees Get Depressed: The Fascinating Science of Animal Intelligence, Emotions, Friendship, and Conservation*. Novato, CA: New World Library, 2013.

Dagg, Anne Innis. *Animal Friendships*. New York: Cambridge University Press, 2011.

De Waal, Frans. *Are We Smart Enough to Know How Smart Animals Are?* New York: W. W. Norton, 2016.
Low, Phillip. "The Cambridge Declaration on Consciousness." Francis Crick Memorial Conference, Churchill College, Cambridge University. July 7, 2012, 1–2.
Safina, Carl. *Beyond Words: What Animals Think and Feel.* Los Angeles: Picador, 2016.
Shanor, Karen, and Jagmeet S. Kanwal. *Bats Sing, Mice Giggle: The Surprising Science of Animals' Inner Lives.* London: Icon Books, 2010.

PART II

A Catholic Case for Animals in Heaven

CHAPTER 3

The Bible on Animals

It comes as a surprise to many that when God first created the world, neither humans nor animals ate meat; all followed a plant-based diet. Paradise was, in today's idiom, vegan.

> God also said: See, I give you every seed-bearing plant on all the earth and every tree that has seed-bearing fruit on it to be your food; and to all the wild animals, all the birds of the air, and all the living creatures that crawl on the earth, I give all the green plants for food. (Genesis 1:29–30).

More familiar to people is Genesis's teaching that God gave humanity dominion over "all the living things" (Genesis 1:28). Though it's commonly assumed that this dominion included permission to eat animals, that's not what's depicted in the Bible. God explicitly allowed humanity to eat flesh only after the flood (Genesis 9), and then as a concession to human sin. The world became something different than what God had originally intended, and God adapted.

The renewal of Catholic biblical studies in the mid-twentieth century encouraged a more historically contextualized reading of texts like these. As today's environmental concerns beg for an ecclesial response, the Church has endeavored to reapproach biblical passages and themes that have traditionally informed its understanding, and sometimes misunderstanding, of the natural world. Three of these appear in the first few chapters of Genesis: humanity as the *imago Dei,* the dominion mandate, and the Fall. These have greatly influenced Catholic attitudes toward animals, and the second of them, the dominion mandate, is likely what Pope Francis had in mind when he said that "we Christians have at times incorrectly interpreted the Scriptures" (*Laudato Si'*, §67). Contemporary biblical scholarship has provided us a more accurate reading of these themes and, in turn, has given us a better understanding of God's hope for the nonhuman world.

That understanding, however, will not be complete until we expand our biblical scope beyond the opening chapters of Genesis. For example, the covenant that God established with Israel is one of the Old Testament's most significant themes. Even though two depictions of it explicitly include animals, the covenant has had little impact on the Church's understanding of the nonhuman world. If we were to allow our theology to be schooled by these animal-inclusive depictions, we would conclude that God's labor in salvation history is intended, somehow, to encompass all creatures. We'll see in the chapter's last section that other themes in the Old and New Testaments teach us the same: God's plan of salvation embraces all of creation.

Interpreting these passages as supportive of animal salvation is not idiosyncratic. As we saw in the previous chapter, many early theologians (the "Church Fathers" in Catholic lingo) held that God's salvific work includes nonhuman creatures because, in their reading, the Bible taught as much. Indeed, the biblical case for a cosmic salvation, one that includes all creation in Christ's salvific labor, is a fairly easy one to make.

Nevertheless, saying that God intends to save all creation does not necessarily mean that God will resurrect specific animals. Perhaps God will decide to resurrect animals, but God could also choose to save them in some other way—for example, by preserving those animals in the divine memory. In this chapter, my primary focus will be on the biblical themes that help us answer the question of whether God intends to save animals. In the next chapter I will continue that discussion while also considering the form that animal salvation will take, whether it will entail their resurrection or something else.

THE *IMAGO DEI*: HUMANITY AS UNIQUE AND UNIQUELY RESPONSIBLE FOR CREATION

The teaching that the human person is made in the image of God, the *imago Dei*, is fundamental to a Catholic understanding of humanity and, by way of contrast, of nonhuman creatures. The doctrine provides the basis for affirming the sacred dignity of every person regardless of individual qualities or characteristics (e.g., health, capabilities, moral character, or stage of life). Genesis 1:26a is the main source for it: "Then God said: Let us make human beings in our image, after our likeness." Though the teaching is found almost nowhere else in Scripture, it is hard to overstate its impact on Christian thought. "Scarcely any passage in the whole of the Old Testament" has generated as much interest "as the verse which says that God created the person according to his image."[1]

What is it about humanity that images God? Theologians do not agree. Catholic answers have traditionally centered on the human intellect and will: We image God because, in a way analogous to God, we are rational and can choose freely. After the Second Vatican Council, however, theologians turned their attention to two other ideas: humanity's distinctive capacity to have a relationship with God (the relational approach) and humanity's role as a divinely appointed caretaker (the functional approach).

According to the relational approach, the human person has a distinctive relationship with God that is not possible for other creatures. Humanity is the image of God because it can hear God's call and respond to it. Through that call, Jesus invites us to be his companions and call God our Father. The capacity for a personal and loving exchange with God is unique to humanity.

The functional interpretation, in contrast, maintains that humanity is the *imago Dei* because it has been given a particular function to perform: The human person is expected to act as God's representative or steward, advancing his goals and desires within the created order. The rationale for this interpretation is that it is consistent with the practices of other cultures during the time of ancient Israel, and it is likely that these practices influenced the Genesis stories. Ancient cultures in the region viewed the king as the local deity's viceroy, the one responsible for promoting the worship of that deity and enacting the deity's commands. In the Genesis version, humanity collectively acts as God's viceroy. We "image" God by representing his interests on earth and enacting his will in the realm of creation.[2]

In 2004 the Vatican's International Theological Commission (ITC) published a document on the *imago Dei* appropriately named "Communion and Stewardship." It was approved by Cardinal Ratzinger, then the head of the Congregation for the Doctrine of the Faith. The document incorporates the above two themes, maintaining that "communion and stewardship are the two great strands out of which the fabric of the doctrine of the *imago Dei* is woven" ("Communion and Stewardship," §25). In discussing communion, the ITC document underscores that the capacity for relationships is essential to what it means to be a human person: "Created in the image of God, human beings are by nature . . . made for one another, persons oriented towards communion with God and with one another." The document's examination of stewardship states that human persons "participate in [God's] work" and "in the divine governance of creation." Such governance must conform to God's "project of love and salvation" ("Communion and Stewardship," §57).

We can adapt these two themes, communion and stewardship, as part of a Catholic case for the inclusion of animals in heaven. Regarding the first theme (communion), we can imagine that God desires communion not only with humanity but also other creatures, in the manner and form that such communion is possible for each of them. All animals share in the capacity for relationship and thus are able to have some type of communion with God.

Regarding the second theme (stewardship), Vatican II's *Lumen Gentium* states that in the age to come, "the human race as well as the entire world, which is intimately related to man and *attains to its end through him*, will be perfectly reestablished in Christ" (*Lumen Gentium*, §48, emphasis added). According to the Church, God has established a salvific link between humanity and the natural world whereby the world is saved in and through humanity. Pope Francis continues this teaching when he says that "all creatures are moving forward *with us and through us* towards . . . God. . . . Human beings, endowed with intelligence and love, and drawn by the fullness of Christ, *are called to lead all creatures back to their Creator*" (*Laudato Si'*, §83, emphasis added). According to these teachings, humanity's stewardship of creation—a role in which we uniquely image God by enacting his will—involves not only caring for creatures on earth but also including them in our journey to God. In God's plan it's not just that animals serve us, but in a way we also serve them, by leading them toward their restoration in the world to come.

HUMANITY'S DOMINION OVER ANIMALS

In Genesis 1:28 God instructs humanity to "have dominion over the fish of the sea, the birds of the air, and all the living things that crawl on the earth." As we saw in chapter 1, this passage has been interpreted at times to justify the exploitation of animals. Though contemporary Catholic thought still maintains that the Genesis mandate permits us to use animals, its understanding of such use is now more tempered and restricted by ethical concerns. This aligns with contemporary biblical interpretations of the text. Most scholars say that dominion means something closer to "rule" and not domination or indiscriminate use. Some go further, arguing that the bestowal of dominion comes with a responsibility to rule over creation in a manner that reflects God's rule—that is, ruling with benevolence and a concern for creation's well-being.[3]

Theologians often use "stewardship" in environmental discussions to capture this sense of dominion as caring governance (we saw an example of this in the previous section). The term helps steer us away from the creation–use mindset associated with the word "dominion" and toward a more creation-centric understanding. Against the temptation to co-opt dominion into a justification for animal and environmental abuse, stewardship highlights the nurturing and nonexploitative rule that God desires us to enact. Genesis 2:15, which depicts God placing Adam "in the garden of Eden, to cultivate and care for it," is often cited as exemplifying this God-given task to steward creation. In a similar vein, Pope John Paul II uses the phrase "minister of God's plan" to describe humanity's relationship with creation (*Evangelium Vitae,* §52), while Pope Francis describes humanity as "protectors of God's handiwork" (*Laudato Si',* §217). Such terms, it is hoped, avoid the negative connotations of dominion while also affirming that God has granted humanity and the Church a distinctive, cultivating task vis-à-vis the rest of creation.

THE FALL AND ITS CONSEQUENCES FOR ANIMALS

Genesis 3 presents the story of the Fall, part of what the website for the US Conference of Catholic Bishops calls the "creation story" of chapters 2 through 11. The story is not a historical account but a figurative narrative meant to convey religious teaching. For example, the story's suggestion that some sort of fall occurred at the beginning of human history is considered church doctrine: "A primeval event . . . took place *at the beginning of the history of man*" and thus "the whole of human history is marked by the original fault freely committed by our first parents" (*Catechism of the Catholic Church,* no. 390, emphasis in original).

As portrayed in these chapters, the world started out as a paradise, but humanity sinned (Adam and Eve ate the forbidden fruit of the tree of knowledge). As a consequence, God allowed the human condition to become corrupted; we now suffer from disease, pain, diminishment, and death, as well as the sinful deeds of others.

What does this have to do with animals? To answer that question, it would help to understand two interpretations of the Fall debated among theologians: an exclusively human Fall and a cosmic Fall. For those supporting a merely human Fall, humanity's sin affected only humanity and left all other creatures untouched. Aquinas, for example, believed that, except for humanity's lot, today's natural world is more or less as it was in paradise. When Adam and Eve sinned, only humanity "fell"—that is, only humanity changed, began to suffer, became vulnerable to natural evils like disease and weather calamities. In contrast, the rest of the world was unaffected by human sin: Lions ate antelope in paradise, and they eat them now (Aquinas, *Summa Theologiae,* I.96.1, ad. 2). Nothing's changed on that front, with one exception: The natural world has ceased to serve humanity as it was supposed to. Unlike in paradise, animals are now disobedient to us (a suitable punishment given that we disobeyed God) and often a threat to us.

Given its assumption that animal violence was part of paradise, an exclusively human Fall is hard to reconcile with the predation-free world of Genesis 1, not to mention the Christian commitment to a peace-loving God. A different interpretation has become more common. In a cosmic Fall, both humanity and the natural world are affected. In contrast to a merely human Fall, a cosmic Fall maintains that animals were also wounded as a consequence of human sin. Lions and antelope lived peacefully in paradise, and we lived peacefully with them. Now neither animals nor humans live in peace. This approach is consistent with the meat-free portrayal of the world in Genesis 1 and also avoids the suggestion that God is responsible for a world cruel to animals. God originally desired a pain-free world for *all* creatures, human and nonhuman, but human sin disrupted that plan.

Evolution has complicated the idea of a primeval fall from paradise, if not upended it. I can't wade into all the issues raised by evolution here except to suggest, without adequately defending, that we can still affirm two ideas taught in Genesis 1–3, even granting an evolutionary framework: First, violence between God's creatures was not part of God's original plan for creation; and, second, the violence presently endured by animals is somehow, in some mysterious way, tied to the advent of human sin.[4]

Church statements do not go into any detail about how the Fall affected animals. Nonetheless, recent papal writings seem to presuppose, if vaguely, a cosmic approach to the Fall, where human sin deeply wounded the entire created order. For example, John Paul II stated that sin "has caused the 'suffering' of man which in some way has affected the whole of creation" (*Dominum et Vivificantem,* §39), and Francis describes how original sin destroyed the harmony among all creatures (*Laudato Si',* §66). The significance for us of a cosmic approach to the Fall is that it ties creation's fate to humanity's: Humanity sinned, and both animals and humans suffered the consequences. Conversely, in line with St. John Chrysostom's arguments, we can hope that when God raises humanity, he will also raise animals. We will see below that this idea of a fundamental solidarity binding together the fates of humanity and the rest of the natural world has significant biblical support.

THE COVENANT AND ANIMALS

For Pope Francis, to be human is to be in relationship with God, with other humans, and with the natural world and all its creatures. Though he rarely references the covenant, it provides the biblical basis for his repeated claim that the God of Jesus Christ desires to be in relationship with his creatures.

As presented in the Old Testament, the covenant refers to the solemn, binding agreement that establishes a relationship between God and the Jewish people. God's covenantal overtures to the Israelite people are central to the Old Testament. (The Hebrew word for covenant, *berith*, appears almost 300 times in the Old Testament.) The New Testament continues this covenantal history by presenting Christ as the one through whom God establishes a new and unbreakable covenant with all of humanity. Thus, appropriately, Christianity uses "testament" to name the two parts of the Bible. (The word comes from the Latin *testamentum* and was intended as a Latin translation of the Greek word for "covenant," *diathēkē*.) In a Christian understanding, salvation history is composed of two covenantal offerings: first to the Jewish people (the old covenant) and then to all humanity (the new covenant).

God's covenantal offer takes different forms in the Old Testament. For example, God makes a covenant with Noah, his descendants, and all creatures after the flood (Genesis 9:8–17); with Abraham and his descendants (Genesis 12:1–3); and with David and the people of Israel (2 Samuel 7:10–13). God's covenant with Moses and the Israelites, however, has been particularly influential for Christianity: "Now, if you obey me completely and keep my covenant, you will be my treasured possession among all peoples" (Exodus 19:5). This Mosaic covenant established a set of divine expectations that God's chosen people were called to fulfill. Although in the Catholic view, God's covenantal offer to the Jewish community was "never revoked by God" (John Paul II, "Audience," April 28, 1999), in its Old Testament form, the covenant failed to achieve God's intent. Thus in order to realize his desire to be in relationship with humanity, God had to intervene in human history and do so radically. The Old Testament prophets (e.g., Isaiah, Jeremiah, and Ezekiel) looked forward to this final intervention (what they often called the "day of the Lord"), and Christianity believes this new era was inaugurated by Christ.

Though Christianity presents Jesus as the realization of the renewed covenant foretold by Jeremiah ("See, days are coming . . . when I will make a new covenant"; 31:31–33), explicit references to the covenant are not common in the New Testament. Nonetheless, the covenant forms the backdrop for much of New Testament theology, and the idea of a covenantal relationship is reflected in themes important to Jesus's preaching, such as reconciliation between God and humanity, peaceful relations among peoples, and, ultimately, the establishment of a just order in the coming of the kingdom of God. And, of course, Jesus's announcement of a new covenant at the Last Supper is preserved at the heart of the Catholic Mass: "And likewise [he blessed] the cup after they had eaten, saying, 'This cup is the new covenant in my blood, which will be shed for you'" (Luke 22:20; see also Matthew 26:27–28 and Mark 14:24).

The covenant has particular importance for St. Paul (himself a Jew). Paul believed that God's covenant with Israel was intended to be a "light to the nations" that broke down walls between peoples—ultimately becoming a covenant that would gather the entire human family (not just the Israelites) into a relationship with God. Paul's preaching against "works righteousness"—the false teaching that we are saved *simply* by our good works—was not intended to promote an individualistic, me-and-Jesus theory of salvation. Rather, Paul wanted to eliminate what he saw as a barrier to non-Jews sharing in God's covenantal offer, the dictates of Jewish law. To do that, he reinterpreted the law's role in establishing our relationship with God. For Paul, having a covenantal relationship with God no longer centers on fidelity to the Mosaic law but incorporation into the universal community established by Christ, that is, the Church.

God's new covenant with humanity is unbreakable, not because the Christian community is sinless any more than the Jewish community was. The foundation of this covenant no longer relies on humanity's fidelity but on the faithfulness of Christ. In Jesus, God has established an everlasting relationship with humanity. He is, as Hebrews 7:22 states, "the guarantee of a better covenant."

With this background, I return to the Old Testament to look at God's covenant with Noah (Genesis 9:8–17). The Noahic covenant is distinctive in that it is explicitly directed to human *and* nonhuman creatures: "I am now establishing my covenant . . . with *every living creature*" (Genesis 9:9–10, emphasis added). The narrative context anticipates the inclusiveness of this covenantal offer. The offer takes place after the story of the flood where God had used the ark to save, *together,* humanity and the animals of the world from destruction. The deliberateness of the inclusion of nonhuman creatures is also underscored by the passage's repetition. Genesis 9 reiterates the phrase "every living creature" four times in order to make its message emphatic: All creatures are to be included in God's covenant.

The book of the prophet Hosea imagines a similarly inclusive covenant. Hosea is beloved among Jews and Christians for the extravagant love that God displays for Israel in the face of Israel's infidelity. Israel breaks the covenant, but God keeps loving. Though angry, God promises that his love, not his wrath, will be victorious. Thus, Hosea looks to a future day (the day of the Lord) when God will repair the broken covenant. Like the Noahic covenant, this covenant will be made with all creation—with humanity and "with the wild animals, with the birds of the air, and with the things that crawl on the ground" (Hosea 2:20).

That two of the covenantal offers include animals is telling. Given the covenant's prominence in Scripture, we must take it seriously when trying to understand God's purposes in creating the world and then saving it from sin. Bracketing animals for a moment, we can observe that God's covenantal overtures signal something startling: that the God of Jesus Christ, who is infinite, absolute fullness and needs nothing else to be complete or happy, wants a relationship with creatures who are, by every measure, unworthy of him. It is an astounding overture of love. To put it more colloquially, God desires to hang out with creatures who are sometimes moody and petty, physically inferior to many other creatures on earth, knowledgeable only about an infinitesimally small part of their world, and destined to quickly fade in ability, looks, and any worldly significance. As Job well put it, the human person is, compared to God, "but a worm, . . . a maggot" (Job 25:6). The reason why God wants a relationship with us isn't rooted in any greatness we've achieved but in God's unfathomable decision to love us and desire our love in return.

We have good reason to hope that God's astonishing and passionate desire to be in relationship extends to animals. As Pope Francis reminds us, "Even the fleeting life of the least of beings is the object of [God's] love," and he "enfolds it with his affection" (*Laudato Si'*, §76). Whatever else we might learn from God's covenantal offers, this much is true: God has an inordinate affection for being in relationship with the creatures he created. The human person has a distinctive place, but given that at least some of the covenantal offers in the Old Testament include animals, it makes sense to hope that God's desire for communion includes creation's varied and multitudinous forms.

THE BIBLE AND GOD'S PLAN FOR ANIMALS

I've suggested that if the animals we have come to know in this life are to join us in the age to come, it is not because of any need or longing on our part but because of what God has accomplished in Christ. There is no pet door or rainbow bridge to heaven that skips over Christ. It is fortunate, then, that the Bible provides ample support for the idea that Christ does indeed include nonhuman creatures in his work.

Before making that case, I should note, candidly, that Jesus never directly addresses the issue of God's ultimate plan for animals. His teachings do not exclude the possibility of their salvation, but neither do they affirm it. His relative silence on the topic is, admittedly, disappointing. Also regrettable for our discussion is that he does not indicate how his exhortations to a radical love for the other might apply to care for animals. Certainly, for some, the fact that he ate fish and, presumably, domestic animals confirms that his exhortations to love were meant only for humans in their relationships with other humans.

And, in at least one case, Jesus seems to act counter to a loving regard for animals: his expulsion of demons into a herd of swine (Matthew 8:28–34, Mark 5:1–20, and Luke 8:26–39). In the story, Jesus allows (Mark and Luke) or commands (Matthew) the demons to leave the afflicted human(s) and enter the swine, which are then drowned, leaving one to wonder whether Jesus had any concern for the perished animals. However, the story's context shows that it's not intended as a teaching about animals. The incident occurs after a series of miracles, suggesting that the purpose of the story is to continue demonstrating Jesus's power over illness and nature. Also, in classic understanding, the expelled demons would have sought out new hosts, leaving Jesus with little choice but to provide an alternative, nonhuman dwelling for the demons.

The story is, fortunately, the exception. Jesus's teachings and practices uphold traditional Jewish beliefs that humans should treat animals with kindness and that God cares for them providentially. These beliefs provide the backdrop for Jesus's tacit support for relieving animal suffering on the Sabbath, over and against legalistic interpretations of the Torah (Matthew 12:11–12; Luke 13:15–16; Luke 14:5) and for his remarks about the providential care that God gives to all creatures (Matthew 6:26–29, 10:29–31; Luke 12:6–7, 12:24).

As to why Jesus was not more explicit in commanding care for the nonhuman world, some speculate that his message focused on countering the evils of the age, which were for the most part intra-human, or that the Bible's message was influenced by its human authors and their interests. But I think the best answer for the dearth of commendations of animal care is that Jesus took as given the Jewish worldview that commended care for animals and imagined them as part of the age to come. The animal-inclusiveness of God's plan was already part of Jesus's heritage and, I believe, generally accepted by him. The story of the fish serving Jesus by providing money to pay taxes (Matthew 17:27) exemplifies the Jewish worldview and Jesus's tacit assumption of it: Animals have their own distinctive roles to play in God's salvific plan.

The biblical case that God's labor of salvation includes animals is compelling—admittedly more so than the narrower issue of whether animals will be resurrected. The strength of the case is due in part to the fact that it is not limited to a few proof-texting quotes or ad hoc appeals but is instead organically part of, and woven into, core biblical themes. We've already seen one example of this integral support for animal salvation: at least two depictions of the covenant, a theme important to both the Old and New Testaments, include nonhuman creatures. Animals are likewise included, explicitly or implicitly, in three other salvific themes: (1) salvation as a new or renewed creation, (2) the harmonious interdependence of all creatures, and (3) the principle of common fate.

When depicting the future age, one of the Bible's favored images is that of a new or renewed creation, one frequently portrayed as teaming with nonhuman life. This is particularly true for the books of the prophets. God encourages the prophet Isaiah, "See, I am creating new heavens and a new earth" (65:17), which Isaiah describes elsewhere as a time when "the wilderness becomes a garden land, and the garden land seems as common as forest" (32:15). Zechariah envisions a future Jerusalem filled with an "abundance of people and beasts in its midst" (Zechariah 2:4). Ezekiel's meditation on the age inaugurated by the Messiah includes animals and crops (Ezekiel 36). In an oft-cited passage, Isaiah foretells a future when all creatures will live in peaceable harmony: "Then the wolf shall be a guest of the lamb, and the leopard shall lie down with the young goat. The calf and the young lion shall browse together, with a little child to guide them" (Isaiah 11:6).

On a couple of occasions, the New Testament also appeals to the image of a new creation: "Then I saw a new heaven and a new earth. The former heaven and the former earth had passed away, and the sea was no more" (Revelation 21:1). *Kainos,* the word used in this passage, is one of two New Testament words for "new." It refers to newness in quality or nature and a renewal of a being; it does not mean "new" in the sense of new in time or not having existed before (which is the meaning of *neos,* the other Greek word for "new"). Thus the new earth referred to here is not a replacement world; rather, the passage's use of "new" has the same meaning as when Paul describes the Christian as a "new creation" (2 Corinthians 5:17)—not a destruction of the old but a renewed transformation of it.

In one place, however, the New Testament does suggest that the old world will be destroyed: "the heavens will pass away with a mighty roar and the elements will be dissolved by fire" (2 Peter 3:10). Though there is some disagreement, the majority of biblical scholars argue that this statement was intended to be taken literally (i.e., it predicts a literal future burning of the world). However, they also observe that the text presents a minority view, one at odds with other biblical statements, especially Romans 8, to which we'll turn shortly. The *Catechism* discounts the destructive aspect of the passage and focuses on the suggestion of a future renewal (see nos. 1042 and 1043, where this passage from 2 Peter is cited). The website for the US Conference of Catholic Bishops likewise notes the oddity of the passage and situates its message within the common imagery of the age: "Although this is the only New Testament passage about a final conflagration, the idea was common in apocalyptic and Greco-Roman thought."[5] Finally, in his reflection on the new heavens and the new earth, John Paul describes 2 Peter 3:11–13 as "symbolic" ("Audience," January 31, 2001). He goes on to criticize "the temptation of those who imagine apocalyptic scenes of the in-breaking of God's kingdom." Such a view, he states, "is opposed by Christ with the quiet coming of the new heavens and the new earth. This coming is similar to the hidden but vigorous growth of the seed sprouting from the ground (cf. *Mk* 4: 26–29)."

Regardless of how we understand its destructive element, the passage from 2 Peter conforms with other passages in its anticipation of the establishment of a future world, one presumably filled with both human and nonhuman creatures. The fact that in creatively and poetically imagining God's renewal of creation in the final age, biblical authors, inspired by the Spirit, regularly envisioned a future that is rich in life, both human and nonhuman, is instructive. They felt that such a diversely alive world is an appropriate end point for God's plan.

The second biblical theme encouraging an animal-inclusive view of salvation is the portrayal of creation as a realm of interconnected creatures that God directs toward a particular end.[6] In the biblical view, all creatures are organically interrelated to one another before a providential God. This view does not conflict with anthropocentrism—humans are still distinct in God's providential concern—but it is at odds with an exclusive anthropocentrism in which humanity is the sole focus of God's creative and providential labors.

Many of the Psalms present the human and nonhuman worlds as one integral realm before the Creator God who brought it into existence and continues to preserve it (see Psalms 24, 33, 104, 136, and 145). "You water the mountains from your chambers; from the fruit of your labor the earth abounds. You make the grass grow for the cattle and plants for people's work to bring forth food from the earth" (Psalm 104:13–14). Similarly, in

Job (38–41), God describes his providential care for creation: He brings "rain to uninhabited land, the unpeopled wilderness . . . [in order to] drench the desolate wasteland till the desert blooms with verdure" (Job 38:26–27). He points with pride to the "Behemoth" (which some speculate to be a primeval monster based on the hippopotamus) and notes "the strength in his loins, the power in the sinews of his belly." "The mountains bring [to the Behemoth] produce, and all wild animals make sport there" (Job 40:15–16, 20). God takes pleasure in these nonhuman creatures and organizes nature such that it provides food for them and spaces for their joyful play.

We noted above Jesus's tacit assumption of the Jewish view that God's providential order extends to all creatures. The author of Ephesians and Colossians gives this a christocentric twist: In Jesus's life, God's providential ordering of creation has entered a new phase. The opening verses of Ephesians state that God's goal in creating, the mystery of God's will for the world, is now revealed in Christ. The substance of this plan is to "sum up" (gathering into one, under one head) "all things in Christ, in heaven and on earth" (Ephesians 1:10). Colossians similarly states that Christ is the end point of creation, that "all things were created through [Christ] and for him," and in Christ "all things hold together" (Colossians 1:16–17). The all-inclusiveness of the language here (i.e., "all things") is intentional: Christ embraces all things, heavenly and terrestrial. Scholars refer to this portrayal of Jesus as the "cosmic Christ." At the end times, Christ will re-form and integrate the entire cosmos and all creatures within it.

The cosmic Christ theme influenced many early church theologians, including Irenaeus, Ephrem the Syrian, and Maximus the Confessor. In keeping with Ephesians and Colossians, their understanding of God's plan is radically christocentric: Christ is not only the *instrumental* means for salvation but also the *end* toward which all creation is destined. In this view, saving humanity from sin is only a partial understanding of what Christ achieved. All of God's labors in history are directed toward something grander and more constructive than simply the correction of primeval fall: God wants to draw all creatures together to himself.

The third biblical theme important for us is what some scholars call the principle of common fate: The destinies of both humanity and the natural world are bound together. This theme is similar to the second, but the emphasis here is not so much on the interrelatedness of all creatures, but on how the nonhuman world's fate is tied to humanity's fidelity or infidelity. All of creation shares in humanity's blessings and its punishments. Creation prospers when humanity is faithful to God and withers when it sins.[7] Thus just as the natural world was cursed to suffer due to Adam's disobedience (Genesis 3:17–19), so will it flourish when God restores the covenant (Isaiah 35). Examples of this principle of common fate appear throughout the prophetic writings (e.g., Isaiah 11:6–9, 43:19–21, 55:12–13; Ezekiel 34:25–31, 36:24–38; Hosea 2:18; and Zechariah 8:12).

Several biblical stories also tacitly affirm the principle. We see this, for example, in the story of Noah's ark. Most of the world's humans and animals are *jointly* destroyed because of the "wickedness of human beings" (Genesis 6:5), while a remnant of both, humans and nonhumans, are *jointly* saved because of Noah, a man whom God found to be "righteous" (Genesis 6:9). Similarly, belief in the intertwined fate of humans and nonhumans helps explain the king of Nineveh's otherwise odd decree that animals share in acts of human penitence. Faced with the prospect of an angry God punishing Nineveh for its sin, the king demanded that all in the kingdom fast, wear sackcloth, and "call loudly to God." The requirement extended to the city's human and nonhuman residents alike (Jonah 3:7–8), so one must imagine even the livestock raising their animal voices to plead for God's mercy. (See also God's joint concern for humans and animals in Jonah 4:11: "And should I not be concerned over the great city of Nineveh, in which there are more than a hundred and twenty thousand persons . . . not to mention all the animals?")

Though Jesus's teachings do not tie together creation's fate to that of humanity, at least one scholar, Richard Bauckham, finds an allusive indication of it in the brief statement of Mark's Gospel: Jesus "was among wild beasts" (Mark 1:13).[8] Interpreted through the lens of Old Testament theology, the passage shows Jesus going out to the desert in order to encounter the creatures of the wilderness and establish his relationship with them (a "friendly companionship," as Bauckham interprets it). The harmonious bond that Jesus establishes between himself and the animals of the wild (which were typically seen as hostile to humanity) is a sign that the messianic age of the peaceable kingdom has begun in the life of animals.

A more explicit embrace of the principle of a common destiny linking humanity and the natural world appears elsewhere in the New Testament.[9] Though one could argue that the cosmic Christ theme of Ephesians and Colossians reflects the principle, a clearer expression of it occurs in chapter 8 of Paul's letter to the Romans, a text that has become particularly important for environmental theology. The text has an eschatological focus (*eschaton* is Greek for the "end"); in describing the condition of humanity and creation as they exist in the present age, the text does so in light of their future status in the end times.

> For creation awaits with eager expectation the revelation of the children of God; for creation was made subject to futility, not of its own accord but because of the one who subjected it, in hope that creation itself would be set free from slavery to corruption and share in the glorious freedom of the children of God. We know that all creation is groaning in labor pains even until now; and not only that, but we ourselves, who have the first fruits of the Spirit, we also groan within ourselves as we wait for adoption, the redemption of our bodies. (Romans 8:19–23)

Paul sets up a contrast between creation's wounded condition in the present age and its liberation from those wounds in the final age, the eschaton. He presupposes the Jewish idea that a salvific solidarity intertwines the fates of the human and nonhuman worlds. For the present age, creation is "groaning." Paul likens those groans to labor pain: They presage the birth of a different age in which creation will share in humanity's deliverance from the suffering of the present.[10]

Unsurprisingly, given that its eschatological claims about creation were at odds with mainstream Catholic assumptions, the passage was generally ignored in church documents before Vatican II. Now, however, the passage has become the go-to text for environmental documents written by church leaders. The text regularly appears not only in papal writings but also in environmental statements by bishops' conferences at the national and regional levels—for example, the Australian Bishops' Committee for Justice, Development and Peace; the Dominican Episcopal Conference; the Guatemalan Bishops' Conference; the Canadian Conference of Catholic Bishops; the United States Conference of Catholic Bishops; the Federation of Asian Bishops' Conferences; and the Conferencia Episcopal Boliviana.

The Romans text offers no specifics about creation's future liberation, and thus these church documents are cautious about claiming too much based on it, beyond a general confirmation that creation is, somehow, suffering in the present and that God intends to save it in the future. In that ambiguity, the passage echoes the present state of Catholic thought on creation, affirming God's intent to include creation in his salvific labors without explicitly identifying what that salvation might mean for creation and the creatures in it.

The passages surveyed above are not cherry-picked from the Bible just because they conveniently support a favored position. Nor is the suggestion that God's salvation includes animals an eccentric idea cobbled together from disparate biblical texts. Rather, it is a teaching deeply embedded within and organically aligned with significant biblical themes that recur throughout the Bible.

CONCLUSION

I have not tried to survey all the passages in the Bible that discuss animals. My goal has been to look at representative biblical passages on animals through the lenses of Christian interpretation and contemporary biblical scholarship. I have focused on passages that have been historically important for shaping Christian interpretation of animals and those that have gained new importance in light of Christian concerns for the environment and the animals within it.

The Bible tells the story of salvation history, God's endeavor to liberate humanity. This story begins with creation and the Fall, then continues with the call of Abraham, the formation of the chosen people, and the prophecies of a future Messiah who will restore peace and justice in Israel. For Christianity, those prophecies are fulfilled in the coming of Jesus Christ and his announcements of the kingdom of God.

The story is anthropocentric and, correspondingly, it generally interprets animals in relation to humanity and its salvation. The three themes in Genesis discussed in the opening sections (the *imago Dei*, the dominion mandate, and the Fall) reflect this framework for understanding animals. All three center on the human person, but they have historically informed Christian attitudes toward animals and the natural world. Contemporary biblical scholars generally affirm the traditional view that these texts grant the human person a privileged status but reject the excessive anthropocentrism that has crept into opportunistic interpretations of them. In church discussions, environmentally friendly themes like communion with creation and the stewardship of it are now used to explain these texts. Consequently, Catholic understanding of human uniqueness and its dominion over creation has been both qualified and enriched.

Scripture provides no precise, literal account of the next life—heaven, to use the more colloquial term. Paul's encouraging note about it is often cited as a reminder of the limits of human knowledge: "What eye has not seen, and ear has not heard, and what has not entered the human heart, what God has prepared for those who love him" (1 Corinthians 2:9, referencing Isaiah 64:3). Nonetheless, the Bible has a number of texts that explicitly show the presence of animals in the age to come. Isaiah's peaceable kingdom (11:6–9) is the most recognized of these.

However, more important are the salvific themes that recur in various forms throughout the Bible and include animals. Often, these are the same themes that inform a Christian understanding of *human* salvation. For example, God's covenant with humanity includes animals in two depictions of it (Genesis 9 and Hosea 2). Other themes also work to jointly illuminate both human and nonhuman salvation: the idea of salvation as a new creation teeming with nonhuman life, the providential integration of all creation in the cosmic Christ of Ephesians and Colossians, and finally the principle of common fate assumed in many Old Testament texts and present in the eschatology of Romans 8. If animals are to join us in heaven, it will be because they are included in the redemption gained in Christ, and these texts and themes justify our hope that this is indeed what God intends to do.

NOTES

1. Claus Westermann, *Genesis 1–11: A Commentary* (Minneapolis: Augsburg, 1984), 148.
2. For an overview of these debates, see Richard J. Middleton, *The Liberating Image: The* Imago Dei *in Genesis 1* (Grand Rapids: Brazos Press, 2005), 93–146.
3. Gordon J. Wenham, *Genesis 1–15*, vol. 1, *Word Biblical Commentary*, ed. David A. Hubbard (Waco, TX: Word Books, 1987), 33.
4. For a discussion of the Fall in light of evolutionary theory, see Raymund Schwager, *Banished from Eden: Original Sin and Evolutionary Theory in the Drama of Salvation*, trans. James G. Williams (Leominster, UK: Gracewing, 2006).
5. For the US Conference of Catholic Bishops' comment on 2 Peter 3:12, see https://bible.usccb.org/bible/2peter/3.
6. See Jamie Tatay, "The Evolution of Catholic Ecological Hermeneutics," *Theological Studies* 85, no. 3 (2024): 379–99.
7. Patrick D. Miller, "Creation and Covenant," in *Biblical Theology: Problems and Perspectives: In Honor of J. Christiaan Beker*, ed. Steven Kraftchick et al. (Nashville: Abingdon Press, 1995), 155–68.
8. Richard Bauckham, "Jesus and Animals II: What Did He Practice?," in *Animals on the Agenda: Questions about Animals for Theology and Ethics*, ed. Andrew Linzey and Dorothy Yamamoto (Urbana, IL: University of Illinois Press, 1998), 49–60, especially 54–59.
9. For example, the New Testament scholar N. T. Wright notes "the scriptural sense" that holds that "the fate of the land is bound up with" Israel's "covenant behaviour." "When Christians are finally redeemed," he goes on to state, "then the land" and "the whole cosmos . . . will be redeemed." Wright, *Pauline Perspectives: Essays on Paul, 1978–2013* (London: SPCK, 2013), 163.
10. For a discussion of this and other interpretive issues, see Cherryl Hunt, David G. Horrell, and Christopher Southgate, "An Environmental Mantra? Ecological Interest in Romans 8:19–23 and a Modest Proposal for Its Narrative Interpretation," *Journal of Theological Studies* 59, no. 2 (October 2008): 546–79.

FURTHER READING

Many of the sources for this chapter's discussions can be found in *All God's Animals: A Catholic Theological Framework for Animal Ethics*. Washington, DC: Georgetown University Press, 2019, 57–67, 78–82, and 101–104.

Church Documents

The Vatican's website has a portal for each pope where their writings, homilies, audiences, and public statements can be found: https://www.vatican.va/holy_father/index.htm.

The *Catechism of the Catholic Church* can be found here: https://www.vatican.va/archive/eng0015/_index.htm.

International Theological Commission, "Communion and Stewardship: Human Persons Created in the Image of God" (April 7, 2004), https://www.vatican.va/roman_curia/congregations/cfaith/cti_documents/rc_con_cfaith_doc_20040723_communion-stewardship_en.html.

Biblical Commentary

Byrne, Brendan. *Sacra Pagina: Romans*. Minneapolis, MN: Liturgical Press, 2007.

Westermann, Claus. *Genesis: An Introduction*. Minneapolis MN: Pilgrim Press, 1992.

Old Testament Themes

Anderson, Bernhard W. *From Creation to New Creation: Old Testament Perspectives*. Reprint edition. Eugene, OR: Wipf and Stock, 2005.

Dubrell, William. *Covenant and Creation: An Old Testament Covenant Theology*. Milton Keynes, UK: Paternoster, 2013.

Habel, Norman C. *The Birth, the Curse and the Greening of Earth: An Ecological Reading of Genesis 1–11*. Earth Bible Commentary. Sheffield, England: Sheffield Press, 2011.

Middleton, Richard. *The Liberating Image: The* Imago Dei *in Genesis 1*. Grand Rapids: Brazos, 2005.

Wiley, Tatha. *Original Sin: Origins, Developments, Contemporary Meanings*. Mahwah, NJ: Paulist, 2002.

New Testament Themes

Galloway, Allan Douglas. *The Cosmic Christ*. New York: Harper, 1951.

Grenz, Stanley J. *The Social God and the Relational Self: A Trinitarian Theology of the Imago Dei*. Louisville, KY: Westminster John Knox Press, 2001.

Habel, Norman C., and Vicky Balabanski, editors. *The Earth Story in the New Testament*. Vol. 5. The Earth Bible. Cleveland, OH: Pilgrim Press, 2002.

Maloney, George. *The Cosmic Christ: From Paul to Teilhard*. New York: Sheed, 1968.

General: The Bible, Creation, and Animals

Bauckham, Richard. *The Bible and Ecology: Rediscovering the Community of Creation*. London: Darton, Longman & Todd, 2010.

Coloe, Mary L., editor. *Creation Is Groaning: Biblical and Theological Perspectives*. Collegeville, MN: Liturgical Press, 2013.

Habel, Norman C., editor. *Readings from the Perspective of Earth*. Vol. 1. Earth Bible. Cleveland, OH: Pilgrim Press, 2000.

Tatay, Jamie. "The Evolution of Catholic Ecological Hermeneutics." *Theological Studies*. Vol. 85 no. 3 (2024): 379–99.

CHAPTER 4

Contemporary Magisterial Views of Animals and Their Salvation

When he was elected pope in 2013, Cardinal Jorge Bergoglio took the name "Francis," the first pope to do so. The motivation for his choice was a plea by fellow Latin American Cardinal Claudio Hummes that he not forget the poor, and in choosing the name Francis—in honor of Francis of Assisi, a saint known for his devotion to the poor—the pope showed his intent to honor that request. Two years later in 2015, the name proved even more apt: With the publication of *Laudato Si'* ("On Care for Our Common Home"), Francis joined his namesake as an advocate for the natural world and the animals in it.

As the first encyclical on ecology, the document unsurprisingly establishes a number of principles for Catholic thinking on creation. However, against the opinions of some detractors, the document's teachings are not new inventions of the Francis pontificate; rather, they continue a shift in Catholic thought about the natural world that stems back to the Second Vatican Council. Through its creative recovery of biblical and patristic sources, the council sought to renew its theology in order to better respond to contemporary needs, and this renewal extended to its theology of nonhuman creation.

In this chapter I examine these developments in magisterial teachings on creation (i.e., the official, formal teachings of the Church). Collectively, they evidence a transition underway toward a more animal-inclusive understanding of Christian salvation.

VATICAN II'S COSMIC ESCHATOLOGY

Over 2,500 Catholic bishops gathered in Rome between 1962 and 1965 for the Second Vatican Council. By Catholic reckoning it was the twenty-first ecumenical (worldwide) council in church history, the first being the Council of Nicaea in 325. The council's teachings reflected shifts already underway in Catholic thought on a number of theological topics and provided a foundation for future developments.

Most significant for us is the council's teaching on eschatology. We've already come across the term, but a more complete definition is merited here. Eschatology refers to theology insofar as it examines the events of the end times; these events include death, purgatory, hell, the Second Coming of Jesus, the resurrection of the dead, the last judgment, and heaven. In the period before Vatican II, the Church's eschatology focused almost exclusively on *humanity's* future. In a significant development of pre-Vatican II views, the council embraced a "cosmic" eschatology: God's salvation is cosmic in scope, and thus the age to come will include the renewal not only of humanity but all creation.[1]

The council's document *Lumen Gentium* (the Dogmatic Constitution on the Church) provides the best-known expression of this in a chapter titled, "The Eschatological Nature of the Pilgrim Church and Its Union with the Church in Heaven" (*Lumen Gentium*, chapter 7). The chapter faced strong opposition and was included only after the majority of the council's participants insisted.[2] Within that heavily contended chapter, we find this striking statement:

> The Church . . . will attain its full perfection only in the glory of heaven, when there will come the time of *the restoration of all things*. At that time the human race *as well as the entire world*, which is intimately related to man and attains to its end through him, will be perfectly reestablished in Christ. (*Lumen Gentium*, §48, emphasis added)

God's salvific labor has a cosmic horizon: Both humanity and the nonhuman world will be restored in Christ. We might suppose that this salvation, as cosmic, will include not only humans but, somehow and in some form, animals, plants, and physical terrains (e.g., mountains, rivers, and prairies). None of the council documents, however, explicitly say as much or provide any details about what the cosmos will look like in that final age, and thus we should be cautious about reading too much into these statements by themselves.

Environmental concerns did not stoke this shift in teaching; those came later. Rather the shift toward a cosmic eschatology grew in part out of a desire to show that Christianity's belief in heaven does not lessen its regard for the world in its present form. Marxism had criticized Christianity on this point, arguing that the Church was unconcerned about the needs of the present world because of its focus on the wondrous glories of the next. Against that view, the council sought to demonstrate its conviction that the present world matters because it is, in its entirety, already linked to its renewal in the final age through Jesus Christ.

Building on the views of early Christian thinkers, the Church began to express more explicitly its belief that the sociopolitical, cultural, and ecological dimensions of human existence in the present age are not mere temporal features irrelevant to the age to come. Through the Spirit's promptings, these dimensions can be healed, developed, and transformed so they begin to align, however proleptically, with the kingdom of God that has been inaugurated in Christ. Though its arrival will ultimately depend on God's intervention and not human labor, the world's future transformation has nonetheless already begun in the present. Thus, the *Catechism* concludes: "Far from diminishing our concern to develop this earth, the expectancy of a new earth should spur us on, for it is here," in the present age, "that the body of a new human family grows, *foreshadowing in some way the age which is to come*" (no. 1049, emphasis added).

If the natural world that we experience now is to be part of this foreshadowing of the next age—a conclusion encouraged by the council's embrace of a cosmic eschatology—then it is not merely an interim fixture. Rather, the natural world will continue to exist in the age to come, in some form, renewed and joined with humanity.

Unfortunately, though the council embraced a cosmic eschatology, it did not address precisely what creation's reestablishment means for the nonhuman creatures living in the present age. Indeed, what little the council did say about the eschatological destiny of the nonhuman world was left ambiguous to avoid contentious issues being debated at the time. Accordingly its discussion of creation's ultimate destiny was comparatively brief. The council's strategic vagueness meant that the task of articulating a comprehensive theology of creation was left to future church deliberations, with the more ecologically concerned popes who came after Vatican II taking up the task: John Paul II, Benedict XVI, and Francis.

MAGISTERIAL TEACHINGS ON ANIMALS BETWEEN VATICAN II AND *LAUDATO SI'*

"The importance of ecology is no longer disputed," Pope Benedict stated to the German Parliament in 2011. "We must listen to the language of nature," he continued, "and we must answer accordingly" ("Address to the Bundestag," September 22, 2011). Benedict regularly condemned humanity's exploitation of the environment. Creation, he maintained, is meant to be the place where the Spirit "comes to meet us," but because of human abuse, "a thick layer of dirt has covered God's good creation" ("Homily," June 3, 2006). He has been called the "green pope" not only because of his sustained critique of environmental abuse but also because of his green practices (e.g., installing solar panels atop the Vatican's Paul VI Audience Hall). He held up the covenant as a model for what a loving relationship with creation can be. Human capabilities, including those made possible by technology, are gifts, he maintained, that we must use well "to reinforce the covenant between human beings and the environment, a covenant that should mirror God's creative love" (*Caritas in Veritate*, §69; see also §50).

Although Benedict's theology of creation was innovative and helped prepare the way for *Laudato Si'*, the foundation for the environmental concerns now common in Catholic magisterial thought was laid by St. John Paul II. An avid hiker and outdoorsman, he was ardent in his regard for creation and deeply concerned about our abuse of it. Humanity, he stated, "is no longer [acting as] the Creator's 'steward,' but an autonomous despot." He warned that humanity must undergo an "ecological conversion" so that the world avoids "the edge of the abyss" ("Audience," January 17, 2001). Humanity's exercise of dominion is not absolute, but must "remain subject to the will of God, who imposes limits upon [humanity's] use and dominion over things" (*Sollicitudo Rei Socialis*, §29). Though humanity occupies a privileged position in God's plan, "this does not authorize [humanity] to take over nature and, much less, to devastate it. On the contrary, [the human person] is called to become a *collaborator of God* in the promotion of creation" ("Angelus," March 24, 1996, emphasis in original).[3]

Environmental themes regularly appear in his speeches, homilies, and writings. Among other places, John Paul II expounded upon a Catholic theology of creation in a series of audiences in 1986 (particularly from April through August). Reflections on creation occurred at several other audiences, including January 17, 2001 (where the pope commended an ecological conversion); January 31, 2001 (where he discussed the new heavens and new earth "inaugurated with the Resurrection of Christ"); February 14, 2001 (where he described creation's recapitulation in Christ as one in which "God and man, man and woman, humanity and nature are in harmony, in dialogue and in communion"); and May 2, 2001 (where he reflected on the "symphony" of creaturely voices praising God). I believe that John Paul is the real forerunner of *Laudato Si'*.[4]

Regarding the question of whether animals will join us in heaven, both John Paul and Benedict continue Vatican II's qualified affirmation. They maintain that, *somehow*, the scope of God's labor in Christ includes nonhuman creation without specifying what exactly that means for animals or, for that matter, any other part of creation (e.g., plants and oceans). We see this ambiguity in Benedict's lauding of the Eucharist as the place where "creation is projected towards divinization" ("Homily," June 15, 2006). It is an inspiring image, but one can wish that Benedict had said more about what exactly creation's "divinization" means. Similarly, though John Paul regularly speaks of creation's restoration, he often adds qualifiers when doing so: "Redemption includes all humanity and *in a certain way* all of creation" (*Dominum et Vivificantem*, §64, emphasis added). Even when his claims are not so qualified, their meaning remains unclear. Thus, after referencing the passage from Romans on creation's liberation (Romans 8:18–30), he states, in an argument that echoes St. John Chrysostom, "Nature itself, since it was subjected to the senselessness, degradation and devastation caused by sin, thus shares in the joy of the liberation achieved by Christ" ("Audience," February 14, 2001). One can commend his view that creation will share in humanity's future joy while still wishing he had said something more about the nature of that joy.

Nonetheless, even if John Paul's teaching on the topic is ambiguous, it appears throughout his writings, and thus it is not a matter of occasional excess or ornamental flourish. Both John Paul and Benedict took seriously Vatican II's teaching that Christ's redemption has a cosmic scope, though both avoided specifying what that redemption might mean for nonhuman creatures.

DETOUR: SALVATION BY PROXY?

Claiming that God intends to save creation, as church teachings have done since Vatican II, is not the same as stating God will resurrect Zach the German shepherd, Blackie the black Labrador, Rocky the moggy, Winter the bottlenose dolphin, Flaco the Eurasian eagle-owl, or Happy the Asian elephant. The idea that God saves individual creatures is a *possible* interpretation of church teachings, but there are others. Here, I'll deviate from our main discussion for a moment to note two alternatives. I do so, first, to argue against them, and second, to anticipate by way of contrast Pope Francis's argument in the next section. He emphasizes the importance of each *individual* creature before God, and that emphasis is difficult to reconcile with these two alternative interpretations, especially when it comes to sentient animals.

The first alternative interpretation is based on the classical view of humanity as a microcosm of creation. Based on the cosmology of Plato's *Timaeus,* widely accepted at the time, classical thinkers understood the human person to contain all the levels of being—or types of existences—within the created order: Humans are rational like angels, have sensory abilities like animals, and live and grow like plants. The human person thus functions as a "microcosm" of creation, representing the entire cosmos in miniature.[5] A microcosmic view was taken for granted by many theologians of the first several centuries and was still a common idea for centuries after.

When Vatican II states that the entire world attains salvation *in the human person,* the claim could be read through a microcosmic lens to mean this: Humanity represents all creation, and when humanity is restored, ipso facto, so too is the rest of creation. Now, if this is understood as saying that creation is saved *only* symbolically through the human person, then it is at odds with what most would consider a real salvation. The world's salvation is instead something more like a salvation by proxy: The entire world is "saved" only in the sense that humanity, as a microcosm, stands in for the rest of creation. Whatever happens to humanity also happens to the rest of creation, though merely symbolically.

A second version of this salvation by proxy is a replacement salvation. God "saves" creation by creating, in the next age, a new order of creaturely beings that are free from the travails endured by creatures in the present age. In this replacement salvation, an entirely new creation replaces the old one. Creation, collectively and as a whole, is theoretically saved, but only by being created entirely anew.

The microcosmic and replacement versions of salvation are both salvation by proxy: The creatures of the present age are saved only in the sense that some other creature who represents them is saved—either the human person or a new, collective replacement of the world as we know it now. In both cases, the individual creatures that suffer and die in the present age are *not* saved, at least not in any kind of commonsense understanding of the term. A proxy salvation is not so problematic for nonsentient creatures (e.g., plants), but it is for sentient creatures, especially those with sufficient cognition to have self-interests, memories of past events, an anticipation of future events, distinctive personalities, and a capacity for joy and suffering. How then might we conceive salvation for such creatures, if not a salvation by proxy?

Any answer necessarily involves a bit of theological speculation given the ambiguity of church teachings on animal salvation. We can begin, however, by observing an obvious point: God saves individual human persons by removing death's sting and resurrecting each of them, not by any sort of proxy salvation. Based simply on this, one might argue that God intends to do something similar for the rest of his creation and resurrect *all* individual creatures—not only the neighbor's cat that likes to sit on our car, the whale with the odd tail markings that we saw in the ocean, and the reddish-brown deer with the big antlers that stopped to eat our flowers, but also the fly we swatted and the basil plant we killed through overwatering.

But that doesn't work so well, at least not from our merely mortal perspective (God might have other ideas). As I noted in the first chapter, it is difficult to imagine, based on what we know, that a creature like a fruit fly might have a subjectivity that could be genuinely resurrected into a new body. All the more so for nonsentient creatures like plants. Sure, God could recreate identical versions of such creatures, but they wouldn't have any connection with the creatures that lived and died in the present age, beyond that of being a physical copy of them.

Thus, I am sympathetic to the variegated approach taken by some theologians. They suggest that though God's salvation is cosmic, inclusive of all creatures, he draws animals to share in eternal life in ways appropriate to each animal. For some animals—horses, cats, seals, and the unexpectedly smart dodoes—salvation could look similar to the resurrection undergone by humans. For creatures with little or no sentience—ants, earthworms, and orchids—resurrection makes less sense. Perhaps God will once again upend our finite understanding and resurrect them also. But if not, God could still, somehow, save them. It might be by recreating the same genetic creature (a clone of a previously existing orchid), or through a proxy salvation (e.g., being renewed in a new form or treasured in the divine memory), or in a manner exceeding our grasp and imaginings.

We do not know the specifics of what salvation will mean for every creature. My claim, however, is that we *can* make sense of what it would mean for God to resurrect at least some creatures—those that are sentient. And so, in my arguments against a proxy salvation, I focus on them.

For a number of reasons, I do not believe salvation by proxy makes good theological or biblical sense for sentient animals. First, the idea that God could save creation via proxy (whether through the human person or a replacement creation) suggests that God does not care for the individual creatures within creation but only for creation in some kind of symbolic or collective sense. This goes against a commonsense understanding of what it means to love. Sentient creatures suffer and die as *individual* animals. One would expect that a salvific God would respond to that type of suffering—that is, to the suffering endured by a particular animal.[6] Reflecting God's tenderness for the particular creature, Scripture tells us that "not one of [these creatures] has escaped the notice of God" (Luke 12:6).

A second reason for rejecting a proxy salvation is that it falls short of the fullness of love revealed in Christ's life, death, *and* resurrection. The culmination of Christ's sacrifice on the cross is the resurrection (i.e., it doesn't end with his death), and that end point discloses what God wants to achieve in Christ. It does not seem fitting, on the one hand, to claim that creation is included in the story of Christ's redemption but then, on the other hand, to deny individual sentient creatures—which, like Christ, suffer and die—the summit of that same redemption: their resurrection in Christ.

Third, the individual animals of the present age manifest a distinct goodness beyond whatever general goodness might be associated with their species' identity. We can hope that God loves this particular and individual goodness. Simply replacing creation with a new version of it would suggest that God does not care for the distinctive goodness and beauty of an animal he once loved into existence. However delightful it would be if God's new creation included a bunch of new dogs and cats, that creation would lack the particular goodness of the individual dogs and cats living in the present age.

We have good reasons to believe that among highly sentient animals, each is endowed with an individualized goodness that can't simply be replaced by that of another animal. Contemporary animal studies confirm that individual animals are distinguished by qualities unique to each of them. Animals—dogs, cats, elephants, great apes, dolphins, and so forth—are individual subjects with distinctive personalities (lazy, aggressive, aloof, nurturing, curious, playful, sweet, shy, mellow, excitable, etc.) and so are more than just interchangeable instances of a species. The naming of pets—which personalizes those animals as distinct, and distinctly beloved, members of our household—is no anthropomorphic projection. It is, rather, a truthful reflection of the animal's creaturely reality: Each companion animal has its own distinctive subjectivity, identity, and character. Because they have distinctive personalities, they correspondingly elicit in us distinctive reactions of enjoyment and affection. We have a particular love for each of these animals because each is good in its own way.

This holds true for any member of a developed species: Each possesses a distinct goodness and personality.[7] The loss of their particular goodness in death is a loss for creation and would impoverish the beauty and goodness of God's new creation. God could, no doubt, fill the aesthetic gap, so to speak, with other forms of creaturely goodness, but it would not be the same goodness that God willed and loved into existence as part of the present order.

Fourth, if we affirm, as I think we must, that the subjectivity of a cognitively advanced animal is something *real*, something that genuinely exists in addition to the animal's bodily reality, then the only way that that particular animal can be saved holistically is if God resurrects it. Anything short of that only restores the animal as an *object* without the mysterious subjectivity unique to it.

This truncated salvation appears in the view of some theologians who hold that God will save animals by preserving them in the divine memory. Memory preservation, however, does not genuinely preserve a sentient animal since in such a "salvation," the animal's sense of self—its consciousness, subjectivity, and so forth—is eternally erased. What is preserved is only an *object* of our thinking, not the mysterious and wonderful reality of that creature's unique sentience.

Finally, God values relationships, and because he does so, we can hope that he also values the creatures that compose those relationships. In chapter 2, I argued that one way of understanding God's plan for creation is the establishment of an everlasting covenant with creation and the creatures in it. The next section will show that Pope Francis has similarly stressed God's desire for a world full of relationships, not only between God and his creatures but also between and among the creatures themselves.

Our contemporary understanding of ecosystems has helped us recognize that the animals of this world are deeply embedded in manifold and complex relationships with human persons and other nonhuman creatures. No creature exists without relating to other creatures. Granted, some of these intercreature relationships lack affection (e.g., the predator/prey relationship) or mutual subjectivity (e.g., insects eating leaves), but I believe that God has an interest in continuing those relationships that do, especially given that they are loving and, in that sense, reflect his own inner life.

We can hope, then, based on what we know about God and his plan for creation, that God's labor in Christ intends to transform both individual creatures and the relationships they have formed with each other. The alternative would be for God to ignore all of the complex exchanges, interactions, symbioses, and interdependencies that already shape the world he created and simply start over. Granted, such a scenario is theologically possible;

God can do what God wants. But it seems more in keeping with the covenantal God revealed in Christ to imagine that he would want to transform and heal these relationships, and thus the creatures within them, rather than initiating some cosmic do-over.

My claim in these arguments is that for sentient animals, a mere proxy salvation is not consistent with what has been revealed about God and his divine interests in creation. However, for other creatures—flower bushes, amoebas, and sea kelp—a proxy salvation is not as problematic. It is hard to imagine that each silverfish has a distinctive personality or a conscious interest in its happiness, and so it is not as troubling to imagine God simply replacing it with another like it or some other creature entirely.

Catholic thought has not traditionally attended to the differences in cognitive capacities among animals (e.g., between a dog and a jellyfish or between a baboon and a slug). The practice of dividing all animals into two categories, the human and the nonhuman, has the consequence of eliding the important differences that exist among nonhuman animals, especially in regard to sentience and intellectual abilities. And with these differences ignored, Catholic thought hasn't considered the possibility that an animal's salvation might take different forms based on those differences.

POPE FRANCIS'S *LAUDATO SI'* AND ANIMAL SALVATION

Pope Francis's *Laudato Si'* is an important advance for a Catholic theology of creation, and two of its insights are particularly significant for us. Before exploring those, however, a word about the authority of the document is warranted, given the debates it has elicited in some quarters of the Catholic world (an indication of just how groundbreaking the document is).

Documents written by popes belong to different categories: encyclicals, papal bulls, apostolic constitutions, apostolic exhortations, motu proprios, and addresses. Among papal writings, encyclicals are second only to apostolic constitutions as having the highest authority for Catholics. Unlike apostolic constitutions, which are typically used to establish church structures and amend church law, encyclicals present a pope's interpretation of church teachings on a particular topic. Encyclicals are not infallible, but they are nonetheless considered formal and authoritative expressions of the Church's beliefs. *Laudato Si'* is an encyclical.

Now on to the document itself. *Laudato Si'* affirms the Church's established view that "all living beings [are not] on the same level" and that human beings have "unique worth" (*LS*, §90). In keeping with previous papal teachings, the pope limits this elevated status by reminding readers that "we are not God" (*LS*, §67) and that we must put "an end to [humanity's] claim to absolute dominion over the earth" (*LS*, §75).

The document, however, develops church teaching on two points relevant to our discussion: first, the importance of relationality, including relationships with nonhuman animals, and second, the care that God has for the *individual* creature.

First, the pope pointedly and repeatedly declares that "everything"—*everything*: humans, animals, plants, all of creation—is "connected," "in communion," "interrelated," and "interconnected" (*LS*, §§16, 42, 70, 76, 91, 117, 120, 137, 138). If the frequency of a theme reflects its importance in a document, then the encyclical can be read as a passionate plea that we recognize our fundamental connectedness to creation and its creatures. For the pope, this interconnectedness of all creatures, human and nonhuman, reflects the God who created them. "The divine Persons are subsistent relations," and since the world is "created according to the divine model," creation "is a web of relationships" filled with "any number of constant and secretly interwoven relationships" (*LS*, §240).[8] The tendency of the world's creatures toward relationships is not just some accident of evolution, but intended by the triune God who created them.

Humans don't just have relationships with other creatures; they *need* such relationships to flourish. To be truly human is to grow throughout our lives within relationships that encompass not only God and our fellow humans but also nonhuman creatures: "The human person grows more, matures more and is sanctified more to the extent that he or she enters into relationships, going out from themselves to live in communion with God, with others and with all creatures" (*LS*, §240). Thus, when Francis speaks of our interconnection with the rest of creation, he means something beyond an ecological interdependency (though he also includes that). Being connected to creation is fundamental to human identity; we are all "linked by unseen bonds and together form a kind of universal family" (*LS*, §89) and are "joined [with the rest of creatures] in a splendid universal communion" (*LS*, §220). Francis describes creation as "woven together by the love God has for each of his creatures and which also unites us in fond affection with brother sun, sister moon, brother river and mother earth" (*LS*, §92). Our connection with other creatures is so profound, so fundamental to who we are, that humanity is wounded by the loss of other creatures and feels "the extinction of a species as a painful disfigurement" (*LS*, §89).

Given its emphasis on the relationality of all creatures, Francis's theology provides additional support for the hope that God's covenant will include animals. God created each creature with a disposition toward relationships, one that God can draw to fulfillment in a covenantal relationship with him. Furthermore, following Francis's logic, it would seem that to be truly human in the next age will require that we continue to live as we do now: in relationship with nonhuman creatures.

Second, and even more important, is the encyclical's emphasis on God's care for the *individual* animal. The pope presents creation not only as a general category to which we all belong but also in terms of the *particularity* of the creatures that compose it. Whereas prior Catholic writings, including those of John Paul II, tended to refer to nonhuman life in collective, abstract terms (e.g., "creation"), Francis's reflections regularly refer to the individual, concrete creature. Thus he tells us that "*each* [creature] must be cherished with love and respect" (*LS*, §42, emphasis added here and in the texts that follow) and that God has a loving plan for "*every* creature" (*LS*, §76). He asserts, "Even the fleeting life of the least of beings is the object of [God's] love, and in its few seconds of existence, God enfolds it with his affection" (*LS*, §77). Furthermore, the fact that the human person is uniquely the image of God "should not make us overlook the fact that *each* creature has its own purpose. None is superfluous" (*LS*, §84). The "importance and meaning of *each* creature" is found "within the entirety of God's plan" (*LS*, §86). The pope appeals to Scripture to exhort us to care for the individual creature: "With moving tenderness," Jesus reminded his disciples "that *each* one of them is important in God's eyes" (*LS*, §96). Finally, Francis describes creation's final movement toward Christ in terms of individual creatures and not creation as a whole: "Eternal life will be a shared experience of awe, in which *each creature*, resplendently transfigured, will take its rightful place" (*LS*, §243, emphasis added here and in the previously cited texts).

Thus the document underscores, repeatedly and emphatically, that God cares for creatures in their *individuality*. Based on this, it seems reasonable that God would want to save creatures in the same way, as individual creatures. Francis's emphasis on the individual creature undermines the idea of a proxy salvation. The logical end point of a divine care that is directed toward *each* animal is not the animal's replacement with another upon death but its restoration in the age to come. In the end times, when God establishes a new heaven and a new earth, God will, we can hope, save Smokey the cat and Fluffy the dog, and not just recreate a bunch of new cats and dogs.

On this question of whether God will raise individual animals to new life, Francis seems to support the possibility even if he does not explicitly affirm it. In an important passage, Francis insists that the salvation offered in Christ includes nonhuman creatures: "The ultimate destiny of the universe is in the fullness of God," and "all creatures are moving forward with us and through us towards a common point of arrival, which is God, in that transcendent fullness where the risen Christ embraces and illumines all things" (*LS*, §83). The reference to "all creatures" (i.e., *individual* entities and not creation in general) reflects the pope's emphasis on the concrete, particular creature instead of creation collectively. Moreover, the phrases "with us" and "a common point of arrival" suggest that the salvific journey for animals and other nonhuman creatures will be shared with humans. That this salvific journey toward the next life is common to humans and nonhumans is further underscored by the text's reference to Christ as the end point for all creation: "Christ embraces and illumines *all things*." Finally, the phrase "through us" invokes the idea of human stewardship discussed in chapter 3: God has invited humans to share in the task of creation's restoration.

One final note. In another development of church teaching, the pope states unequivocally that the value of plants and animals is not measured by their service to humanity: The "ultimate purpose of other creatures is not to be found in us" (*LS*, §83). With this statement, the pope undercuts the argument that there will be no animals in heaven because humans will not need them. Though service to humanity may well be *part* of the reason why animals were created, their telos, the end toward which they are ultimately directed, is not found in such service. One of the reasons God created nonhuman creatures, according to Francis, is because they reflect God's glory and give him praise. And we can imagine that if God loves animals because of the glory they reflect and the praise they give, then he will want them to continue reflecting such glory and offering such praise in the life to come.

THE *CATECHISM* ON ANIMALS

Catholics have good reasons for hoping that the animals we know in this life will join us in the next. This is not an official teaching of the Church, even if the logic of Francis's theology points in that direction. I believe that Catholic teachings on animals are currently in transition; the Church is striving to be faithful to the received tradition while also developing that tradition in a way that incorporates contemporary theological insights and is more attuned to our responsibilities as kind and merciful stewards of creation.

Tensions in the *Catechism*'s teaching on animals reflect this state of flux; it is a mixture of the anthropocentric emphases that dominated during the modern period (i.e., animals have duties toward humanity) and a more Gospel-inspired exhortation to treat animals kindly. The two approaches are not entirely integrated in the document. Since the *Catechism* has an official status for the Catholic community, I close this chapter with an examination of its discussion of animals to complete our overview of the Church's doctrine on animals.

The *Catechism of the Catholic Church,* a project initiated by John Paul II, gathers all the fundamental teachings of the Catholic Church into one volume. It comprises 2,865 numbered paragraphs and was first published in 1992 (English, 1994). It is a helpful go-to reference for determining whether or not a particular claim aligns with formal church teaching. The doctrines on creation presented in the *Catechism*'s 2018 edition remain unchanged from the 1997 edition (and so, for now, *Laudato Si'* has not impacted its statements).

Two sections of the *Catechism* are relevant for our topic: the section on the world's final transformation at the end of time (nos. 1020–1065) and the section on the ethical treatment of animals (nos. 2415–2418). Here, I'll focus on the second section, reserving the first section for chapter 6, where I'll offer an animal-inclusive sketch of the world's final transformation.

The section has this to say about our treatment of animals:

> **2415** The seventh commandment enjoins respect for the integrity of creation. Animals, like plants and inanimate beings, are by nature destined for the common good of past, present, and future humanity. Use of the mineral, vegetable, and animal resources of the universe cannot be divorced from respect for moral imperatives. Man's dominion over inanimate and other living beings granted by the Creator is not absolute; it is limited by concern for the quality of life of his neighbor, including generations to come; it requires a religious respect for the integrity of creation.
>
> **2416** Animals are God's creatures. He surrounds them with his providential care. By their mere existence they bless him and give him glory. Thus men owe them kindness. We should recall the gentleness with which saints like St. Francis of Assisi or St. Philip Neri treated animals.
>
> **2417** God entrusted animals to the stewardship of those whom he created in his own image. Hence it is legitimate to use animals for food and clothing. They may be domesticated to help man in his work and leisure. Medical and scientific experimentation on animals is a morally acceptable practice if it remains within reasonable limits and contributes to caring for or saving human lives.

> **2418** It is contrary to human dignity to cause animals to suffer or die needlessly. It is likewise unworthy to spend money on them that should as a priority go to the relief of human misery. One can love animals; one should not direct to them the affection due only to persons.

Some observations. The *Catechism* situates the above injunctions within its reflections on the seventh commandment: "You shall not steal." Thus it presents the Church's approach to animals within a framework of *property* that God has given humanity. People must use this "property" (i.e., plants and animals) in a just and prudential fashion, but it is still theirs to use.

Also, in keeping with recent teachings, the first paragraph (no. 2415) holds that humanity was given dominion over animals while also noting that God set limits to this dominion. These limits, however, have little to do with a direct interest in the well-being of the animals themselves. Instead the limits God imposes are meant to protect human interests: Since God gave animals as property to all humanity—past, present, and future—animals must be shared with other humans in accord with that universal purpose. Thus no single part of humanity or generation of humans can deplete this animal wealth so that it is not available for other humans or for future generations.

Skipping no. 2416 for now, we can note what seems to be a non sequitur in no. 2417. After stating that "God entrusted animals to the stewardship of those whom he created in his own image," the *Catechism* concludes: "*Hence,* it is legitimate to use animals for food and clothing" (emphasis added). The *Catechism*'s logic here stumbles a bit. It appeals to the fact of our stewardship of creation and then, on that basis, concludes that we can eat animals. However, as we saw in chapter 3, when God first gave us dominion (Genesis 1), we were *not* permitted to use animals for food. I believe God does allow us to use animals for food and clothing, but that permission does not derive simply from our stewardship of creation, at least not as described in the first chapters of Genesis.

The tone in no. 2416 is different. It not only encourages animal care and kindness, but says that we "owe" animals such kindness. The text points to St. Philip Neri as an example. The saint was famous for his compassion for animals, abstaining from all meat, refusing to swat flies, and releasing captured mice. The clause also reminds us that animals have a purpose besides serving humans: They bless and give God glory.

This paragraph appeals to a different standard for our treatment of animals than that given by the other paragraphs: It makes no reference to human need but states that we are to care for animals because God cares for them. One could argue that the *Catechism*'s basis for animal care in this clause *has* to change from the one found in the section's other paragraphs. Viewing animals merely as property for human use, as the other clauses do, cannot by itself explain why we should treat them with kindness. If they were *merely* property, we would not owe them anything more than an obligation to use them well—effectively, efficiently, responsibly. Thus it is understandable that when this section turns to encourage us to be kind to animals, it does so *not* based on their identity as our property or our dominion over them, but on the basis of something else: the animals' relationships with God. There is a tension here—not necessarily insurmountable, but a tension nonetheless—between understanding animals as property to be used and viewing them as creatures cared for by God and saintly Christians.

Also reflecting this tension between using animals and being kind to them is the last clause. The *Catechism* doesn't clarify what it means to spend money on animals "that should as a priority go to the relief of human misery." If we are to care for animals because God cares for them, then spending money on them is legitimate and generally necessary. But based on this paragraph's argument and given humanity's virtually limitless needs, one could argue that any money spent on animals is wrong; such money should have been redirected toward relieving human suffering. Given the choice between, say, spending money on medicine for one's dog and sending that money to buy medicine for an isolated village, it seems that the human villagers must win out.

We can assume that the *Catechism* is not saying as much, given that the Church has never condemned pet ownership or the basic expenditures that go with it. But the text pulls us in different directions and does not provide guidance on how to resolve the tension between our God-given permission to use animals, within limits, and our obligation to treat them with saintly kindness.

CONCLUSION

Catholic teaching has become increasingly explicit that God's salvific work in Christ includes, *somehow*, nonhuman creation. The "somehow" is key; it provides a veil of obscurity over church teachings on animals, allowing the Church to say something without saying too much. Since official teachings do not say what precisely Christ's salvific offer means for the animals of the present age, my discussion going forward will necessarily become more speculative, though not entirely so. I believe that my argument is based on Catholic commitments, good theological reasons, and the teachings of recent popes, especially those of Pope Francis.

Denying salvation to the sentient animals that have lived in this present age goes against the logic of God's redemptive work. God loved individual creatures into existence. God is the God of relationships and wants to enter into a covenant with all creatures. It would be odd for God, who loved the present world into existence, to discard the old and simply create a new version of it. The animals that exist here and now are part of our lives, part of human history; sometimes they have shaped our lives in profound ways. Our relationships with them have been life-giving to us and, we hope, to the animals themselves. Preserving one side of creaturely relationships (the human part) while abandoning the other (the nonhuman part) seems contrary to the covenantal hopes that God achieved in Christ.

I read Pope Francis as advocating an inclusive view of the resurrection in his theology of creation. He repeatedly reminds us that God cares for *each* creature—not just for creation in general but for the concrete, individual creatures within it: Floki the corgi, Ellie the golden retriever, Kathy the dolphin, and Grizzly 399 the Wyoming brown bear. Given God's concern for the individual animal, it is arguable that God would likewise want to save that particular animal and not some representative or proxy of it.

I noted, nonetheless, a limit to this hope: God may decide to save creatures of primitive cognition (e.g., insects)—which do not, it seems, have the subjective wherewithal to be resurrected—in a manner different from more developed animals. Again, however, my intent is not to exclude that possibility or argue for what God cannot do. My suggestion is only that for many of the animals that we've come to know, it *does* make sense to hope that God can grant them what he grants humanity: resurrection.

NOTES

1. At Vatican II, "eschatology was brought from the margins to the center of Christian thought and was linked with the key doctrines of the Christian faith." Peter C. Phan, "Roman Catholic Theology," in *Oxford Handbook of Eschatology*, ed. Jerry L. Walls, Oxford Handbooks Series (Oxford: Oxford University Press), 217.
2. For a discussion of this debate, see Candido Pozo, *Theology of the Beyond*, trans. Mark A. Pilon, 5th ed. (Staten Island, NY: Society of St. Paul, 2009), 97–130.
3. I discuss developments in Catholic thinking about creation in "What's the Plan? Deciphering the Shifts and Ambiguities in Recent Papal Teachings on Creation's Eschatological Destiny and Its Temporal Care," *Horizons* 48 (2022): 267–301.

4. See Peter C. Phan, "Pope John Paul II and the Ecological Crisis," *Irish Theological Quarterly*, 60, no. 1 (1994): 59–69.
5. See Rudolf Allers, "Microcosmus: From Anaximandros to Paracelsus," *Traditio: Studies in Ancient and Medieval History, Thought, and Religion* 2 (January 1944): 319–407.
6. A criticism of *Laudato Si'* is that it doesn't do enough to attend to animal suffering. See Denis Edwards, "'Sublime Communion': The Theology of the Natural World in *Laudato Si'*," *Theological Studies* 77, no. 2 (June 2016): 377–91.
7. See Barbara J. King, *Personalities on the Plate: The Lives and Minds of Animals We Eat* (Chicago: University of Chicago Press, 2017).
8. Celia Deane-Drummond explores the theme of interconnectedness in her "A New Anthropology? *Laudato Si'* and the Question of Interconnectedness," in Laudato Si' *and the Environment: Pope Francis' Green Encyclical*, ed. Robert McKim (New York: Routledge, 2020), 189–201.

FURTHER READING

Many of the sources for this chapter's discussions can be found in chapter 3 of *All God's Animals: A Catholic Theological Framework for Animal Ethics*. Washington, DC: Georgetown University Press, 2019, 95–102.

Church Documents

The most significant Catholic Church documents are available on the Vatican website, www.vatican.va.
Documents from the Second Vatican Council can be found here: https://www.vatican.va/archive/hist_councils/ii_vatican_council/index.htm.
The Vatican's website has a portal for each pope where their writings, homilies, audiences, and public statements can be found: https://www.vatican.va/holy_father/index.htm.
The *Catechism of the Catholic Church* can be found here: https://www.vatican.va/archive/eng0015/_index.htm.

Contemporary Theology and Animals

Clough, David. *On Animals*. Vol. 1. *Systematic Theology*. London: T&T Clark, 2012.
Linzey, Andrew. *Creatures of the Same God*. New York: Lantern, 2009.

Catholic Thought on Creation

Benedict XVI. *The Garden of God: Toward a Human Ecology*. Translated by Maria Milvia Morciano. Washington, DC: Catholic University of America Press, 2014.

Irvine, Kevin W. *A Commentary on* Laudato Si': *Examining the Background, Contributions, Implementation, and Future of Pope Francis's Encyclical*. New York: Paulist, 2016.

John Paul II. *Following St. Francis: John Paul II's Call for Ecological Action*. Edited Marybeth Lorbiecki. New York: Rizzoli Ex Libris, 2014.

Martin, Terry. *Animals in Heaven? A Catholic Pastoral Response to Questions about Animals*. Eugene, OR: Wipf and Stock, 2024.

Miller, Vincent J., editor. *The Theological and Ecological Vision of* Laudato Si': *Everything Is Connected*. New York: Bloomsbury, 2017.

PART III

Constructing a Catholic Theology of Animals

CHAPTER 5

A Trinitarian Theology of Animal Salvation

"If animals can go to heaven, they can also go to hell." Anyone who reads enough Catholic blogs about animals will eventually come across some version of this. It's amusing on the surface but an odd claim theologically. In the Christian understanding, there's only one way that someone (or something) goes to hell: the free decision to reject God. And, as far as we know, animals don't have that capacity.

Another version of the argument, however, raises a more serious challenge: Animals can't say "yes" to God, and so they can't be in heaven. Other critiques follow a similar pattern. They argue that the idea of animals in heaven entails corollaries that are nonsensical and, therefore, the original idea itself is wrong. How can a dog confess faith in Jesus? Won't heaven be overrun with nasty insects? Can any animal participate in the beatific vision?

The weakness of these arguments is that they move straightforwardly from humans to animals, foisting upon animals a theological structure meant for humans without any adjustment. It's like bathing dogs in wonderfully scented shampoos: Those products might be fine for smell-challenged humans, but they're a disaster for animals with olfactory superpowers. Same thing theologically: What works for humans doesn't necessarily work for animals.

The best way to address these challenges is to prove the contrary, that it is not silly but makes sound theological sense to believe that animals will be saved and join us in heaven. Doing so, however, requires a creative turn in our discussion: constructing a theology that translates doctrines on human salvation into ones that work for animals. The undertaking will necessarily be speculative in that it leads us beyond formal church teachings. My goal in this and the next chapter is only to show that we *can* make sense of two ideas, animals being saved and their joining us in heaven, not to suggest that mine is the best or only way of doing so. Here I propose a way of understanding animal salvation and do the same for the idea of animals in heaven in the next chapter.

Finally, a heads up to the reader: The argument requires we examine some heavy theological theory—an unavoidable labor given that the doctrine of the Trinity's involved. We'll get through it.

ANIMAL SALVATION IN A TRINITARIAN CONTEXT

The challenge raised by critics that the idea of Christ saving animals makes no sense is important to address. My claim has been that if animals are to join us in heaven they must, like humans, participate in God's salvific plan. This is the "through Christ alone" argument: The liberating gift of Christ must be extended to animals for them to be included in God's kingdom. There is no pet door or rainbow bridge to heaven that skips over Christ. Thus, if critics are right that animals can't be drawn into Christ's salvific achievement, then their conclusion is correct: The animals of the present age will not be in heaven.

But I believe their argument is wrong. To defend that conviction, I'll appeal to a core belief of Christianity, that God is the eternal exchange of the three divine Persons. It's a particularly auspicious doctrine for my purposes as it allows me to construct a theory of animal salvation based on God's desire for relationships. Some theologians see in God's triune life a model for human relationships,[1] and Pope Francis extends that trinitarian standard to all creatures: "Creatures tend towards God, and in turn it is proper to *every living being* to tend towards other things, so that throughout the universe we can find any number of constant and secretly interwoven relationships" (*Laudato Si'*, §240, emphasis added). God desired to create a world of "interwoven relationships" that reflects his own divine life, and, we can argue, when God turns to save the world, he will do so by healing all those relationships that have been wounded by sin and draw the creatures within them to fulfillment in him.

To make this case, I'll follow Hans Urs von Balthasar's understanding of the Trinity and its role in human salvation.[2] Balthasar was one of the most important Catholic theologians of the twentieth century and was held in high esteem by both Pope John Paul II (who had intended to name Balthasar a cardinal before Balthasar's unexpected passing) and Pope Benedict XVI (who as Cardinal Ratzinger gave the homily at Balthasar's funeral). Balthasar is a good candidate to guide us. Against the mainstream view of his time, he argued passionately that God's redemptive plan includes animals.[3]

The Trinity

The doctrine of the Trinity is a mystery in a formal sense. It's not a puzzle we haven't figured out yet and is just pending more information or further insights. It essentially exceeds our ability to understand. Nonetheless, without hoping to fully explain the mystery, the Church is committed to a few fundamentals about the doctrine. God is one and yet also three Persons. God is not three gods but rather one God in absolute unity. Nor is it the case that the three Persons together compose the one God, as if there are three parts to God. The Father is God, the Son is God, and the Holy Spirit is God. Neither can the three Persons be explained by saying God is one deity who acts in three different ways or modes. God is absolutely one God in three divine Persons. The Father is the eternal origin of the Godhead, the Son is eternally begotten from the Father and returns all to the Father, and the Holy Spirit proceeds (eternally, without a beginning or end) from the Father and the Son. Three fully divine Persons; one absolutely united Godhead. A mystery.

The Church maintains that our language about God is always analogous: The words that we use to describe God (triune Persons, the Father begetting the Son, the Father sending the Spirit, etc.) do not mean the exact same thing as they do when we describe human or earthly realities. They are *analogous* terms. They are descriptions that we use neither in a univocal sense (as if descriptions of a person as "loving" or "generous" mean the same thing when applied to God) nor in an equivocal sense (as if descriptions of a person as "merciful" or "compassionate" mean something completely different when applied to God). Some correspondence in meaning exists between the words we use to describe God (loving, generous, etc.) and the reality of that which we call God, and yet, nonetheless, all descriptions of God fall short.

How then can we know anything about God, given that God is a mystery about whom all language is inadequate? Because God has revealed himself to us in human history and, ultimately, in Jesus Christ. We could not have known God without this revelation. The God revealed in the biblical story that culminates in Jesus Christ is what theologians call the "economic Trinity": God insofar as God labors in the world and reveals himself through his acts in the world. This is distinct from what theologians call the "immanent

Trinity": God's life within the triune Godhead. They are, of course, the same God; the economic Trinity (the God who acts in the world) reveals the immanent Trinity (God in God's inmost Self).

In short, (1) God is one God in three divine Persons; (2) God is absolute mystery and always exceeds human understanding (in Augustine's language, *si comprehendis, non est deus*; if you understand, it is not God); (3) though descriptors of the creaturely realm can never be applied univocally to God, they must be used nonetheless as analogous terms to describe God; and (4) the economic Trinity (God as God labors in human history) reveals the immanent Trinity (God's internal life within the Godhead).

The Trinity, Jesus, and Human Salvation

Now on to Balthasar's theology. For Balthasar, Scripture compels us to apply, albeit analogously, the language of interpersonal relations to the triune life of God; the Father, the Son, and the Holy Spirit are Persons in relationship with one another. Interpersonal and even dramatic language (e.g., the Father loves the Son; the Son surrenders everything over to the Father) is necessary in order to portray the vital and dynamic mystery of the love that has been revealed in Christ. Thus Balthasar relies on vibrant descriptions for God's interior life. The language is metaphorical, but it provides a helpful image for our mortal minds as we try to grasp what is finally ungraspable.

Balthasar emphasizes that God in God's interior life is not best understood as an unmoving and static Godhead, but, using a different metaphor, an eternal dance of divine exchange. The fullest revelation of this dramatic, triune life occurs in the death and resurrection of Christ. In these saving events, an interchange occurs between the Father and the Son. On the cross, having received everything from the Father, the forsaken Son now returns everything, including the gift of his own life, over to the Father. The Father accepts the Son's gift of himself, resurrecting him by the power of the Holy Spirit. This interchange between the Father and the Son reveals the *shape* of divine love: It is self-giving love for the other. The mutual self-giving love between the Father and Son shows that God is, in God's very Self, the One who gives and receives.

How does this allow God to save humanity? Three points. First, in Catholic understanding, the very fact that God became human affects all of humanity. We're not used to thinking in this way, but Catholic thought has long held that a fundamental ("ontological") bond ties all of humanity together. Thus, when Adam and Eve fell, all humanity fell with them. The Incarnation begins to reverse that. In becoming incarnate (i.e., enfleshed as a human person in the birth of Jesus), the Second Person of the Trinity effectively joins himself with all of humanity. And because one of us is the Son of God—because the Son became human like us—all of humanity is, in turn, joined to God.

Second, Jesus stands in for us in our sinfulness. In becoming human, the Second Person of the Trinity accepts the weight of human sin, though sinless himself: "For our sake he made him to be sin who did not know sin" (2 Corinthians 5:21). On the cross the Father confronts sinful humanity in the person of his beloved Son. The Father accepts Jesus's self-sacrificial offer on the cross: He raises Jesus. In doing so, the Father accepts and draws to himself not only Jesus but all of humanity, since humanity is joined to the God-human Jesus Christ.

Third, in explaining the relationship between the Father and the Son, Balthasar introduces the metaphor of an acting "space" existing between them. He uses the image to convey imaginatively the idea that there is a relational distinction between the Father and the Son, and thus the connection between the Father and the Son should not be imagined as a compressed, frozen unity, but something more like an acting space in which dramatic interchange between them occurs.

These three points come together in Balthasar's theory of salvation. For all eternity, the Father and Son have related to each other in what Balthasar has imagined as an acting space. In the Father's acceptance of Jesus (representing sinful humanity), this relational space is transformed, expanded, so that it now includes all humanity. God has invited the human person into the very acting space of God's own life; in the Father's embrace of the God-human Jesus Christ, the Father now embraces all of humanity. And, correspondingly, humanity is now, in and with Christ, turned to the Father as our Father. To put it more colorfully, we are Jesus's "plus one" at a divine party none of us deserves to attend.

Balthasar is not without his critics. For some, his discussion of God's triune life makes claims that exceed what can be known through revelation. A theologian friend once quipped, "Balthasar wanders around the inner life of the Trinity the way I walk around my apartment." I understand the sentiment, though it's not my own view. All metaphors are limited, but I believe Balthasar's image of an acting space within God is helpful for approaching the mystery of human salvation.

Balthasar's image is powerful, to my mind at least, for another reason. It offers a way of addressing an issue that has long been debated among theologians: Did Jesus *have* to die? At the real risk of eliding tensions and oversimplifying theological issues, Balthasar's answer is that God had to become a God who welcomes sinners. That is, in order for God to be in relationship with humanity, God had to "change" and become a God who can embrace what is not God. On first glance, this seems a paradox: the holiness of God becoming entangled with the sinfulness of humanity. But in Jesus Christ and through his death and resurrection, God—who is, as we saw, eternal self-giving and other-receiving—has made the impossible possible. The Son's death on the cross expresses the radical and complete gift of himself to the Father. The Father accepts the Son's perfect self-gift, and as a result, the eternal relationship between the Father and the Son now stretches to include humanity, to include we who are sinners. With the Father's embrace of the sinless God-human, Jesus Christ, sinful humanity is also lifted up and divinized *in and with* Christ. And, *in and with* Christ, humanity now faces the Father as our Father. This new relationship already begins in our life now and will be brought to its fullness in the age to come.

THE HOLY SPIRIT AS SALVIFIC BOND

One of the biblical themes discussed in chapter 3 holds that a salvific bond exists between humanity and nonhuman creation. As God draws humanity to himself, he also draws all of creation (see Romans 8:19–23). We saw in the last chapter that Vatican II taught the same: The "entire world . . . is intimately related to man and attains to its end through him" (*Lumen Gentium*, §48). Pope Francis continues the teaching but with his characteristic emphasis on *individual* creatures, not the "world" in general: "All creatures are moving forward with us and through us towards . . . transcendent fullness" (*Laudato Si'*, §83). The one integral piece remaining to make sense of how this bond between humanity and creation becomes salvific is the role of the Holy Spirit.

Before turning to consider the Spirit's role, we should note a basic theological maxim to follow when discussing the trinitarian Persons. The works of God are always one—the Father, Son, and Spirit act in absolute unity. The terms we use to describe their acts in the world, like all language about God, are inadequate; any implication that each Person of the Trinity has an independent task performed separately from the other Persons is wrong. Thus, in giving grace, the Holy Spirit does not act as a divine agent doing his own thing. God's actions in the world are always one: Father, Son, and Spirit.

Nonetheless, the tradition has allowed us to associate certain forms of God's activity in the world with one of the Persons of the Trinity. Theologians describe this way of speaking as "appropriation." Though God is one and God's labor is also one, the Christian tradition has associated certain roles with one or other of the Persons of the Trinity. Thus, when we say that Christ "saves" us, it is a case of appropriation: We are associating a particular work in the economy of salvation with one of the Persons of the Trinity. Ultimately, salvation is the united work of all the Persons of the Trinity, even if the act of saving humanity can be appropriated to Christ and the act of drawing the person to unity with God appropriated to the Holy Spirit.

When Christians imagine the Father and the Son acting, they generally attribute to them some kind of personal agency. That is, in our thinking about the Father and the Son, Christians will regularly speak about them *doing* things (e.g., speaking and acting). In that sense, we might think of the Father and the Son as "agents," individual subjects of intentional activity. The Christian tradition has allowed this but only with a pointed caveat: We must understand these images analogously. It would be wrong, for example, to attribute to the Father an isolated, individual consciousness, one separated from that of the Son, or to believe that they are acting as independent agents. Though Scripture encourages us to imagine the triune Persons in ways analogous to that of individual human persons—the Father speaks, the Son acts—we must also acknowledge the ultimate inadequacy of such language.[4]

What about the Holy Spirit? Participants at the Second Vatican Council encouraged renewed attention to the work of the Spirit, emphasizing the Spirit's distinctive role while continuing to underscore the Spirit's absolute unity with the one salvific work of God.[5] We are allowed to imagine the Holy Spirit as a personal agent of God's presence in the world—the Spirit, if you will, *does* things, like the Son and the Father. Thus, Pope Francis speaks of the Spirit as the "Protagonist," the One who leads the Church in its mission and guides the Church as it creatively responds to new circumstances ("Audience," February 22, 2023).

In Catholic understanding, the Holy Spirit is the One who "proceeds" (flows forth) from love of the Father and the Son and also acts as the bond between them. The Spirit is both: loving Bond and divine Person. Balthasar describes this twofold aspect of the Spirit as the *objective* bond between the Father and the Son and the *subjective* (or personal) expression of their love. We can imagine, however inadequately, the Spirit as both object and subject within the triune life of the Godhead; he is the loving Bond between the Father and the Son (object) and the personal Agent of that bond (subject).[6]

This describes the Spirit within what theologians call the immanent life of the Trinity. As I noted above, most contemporary theologians emphasize that when God labors in history—for example, in sending the Son and the Spirit—God's actions in the world reflect the interior life of the Trinity. What the Spirit and the Son do in the world (the economic Trinity) continues the life they have within the Godhead (the immanent Trinity). The economic Trinity (God insofar as God acts in the world) reflects and reveals the immanent Trinity (God in God's own self).[7]

This is some heavy theory, but I have a reason for asking readers to trudge through it. It provides the background for a point critical to Balthasar's approach to *human* salvation and will, as we'll see in the next section, be important for my theory of *animal* salvation: The activity of the Spirit in human history continues the dual activity of the Spirit within the Godhead. That is, within God's triune life, the Spirit acts as personal Agent of divine love and the Bond of that love. When the Spirit labors in the world, the Spirit continues this twofold role he has within the Godhead. The Spirit (1) acts with and within each human person (the Spirit acts as subject-Agent with us) and (2) draws the person into God's life (the Spirit acts as the object-Bond that ties us to God). Thus, on the one hand, the Spirit works within graced human persons, helping them to act in Christlike ways; in this sense the Spirit is co-Agent with the person. But, on the other hand, the Spirit also acts to join those persons to God, and in this sense the Spirit is the loving Bond between God and the human person.

A reminder of the maxim noted above: The work of the Spirit is utterly united with that of the Son, and in lifting up all persons into a graced relationship with God, the Spirit does not do something different or apart from the work of the Son but rather continues that same work. In Balthasar's apt phrase, the Spirit "liquefies" Christ. Jesus Christ existed as a concrete, historical person, living in a particular region of the world during a particular moment in time. The Spirit expands, liquefies, the saving mission of the concrete, historical Jesus Christ so that it is no longer limited to a particular time and place but embraces all times and places—and, I will argue shortly, all creatures.

Salvation then is effected by what the tradition has referred to as the "Two Hands" of the Father: Jesus, in his life, death, and resurrection, establishes the conditions for God's universal saving offer, and the Holy Spirit acts as the Agent and Bond who effects that salvation in the individual creature.

The Trinity and Animal Salvation

Though Balthasar doesn't pursue the possibility, we can expand his metaphors of a salvific space within the Trinity and the loving bond of the Spirit to help us understand the salvation of animals.[8]

The argument for that adaptation begins with the salvific bond that exists between humanity and all creation. Incorporating this salvific bond within Balthasar's trinitarian framework, I suggest that in the eschaton (the end times) animals, so linked to and bonded with humanity through the person Jesus Christ, will join humanity in the relational "space" that Christ has established within the Trinity.

We can now address a criticism raised above: Animals are unable to freely say yes to God's offer of salvation and thus can't be saved. In response I offer two observations and then return to the above framework to situate animals within it. First, every creature, no matter how primitive, acts just by being what it is and in doing so, praises God: "Let everything that has breath give praise to the LORD" (Psalm 150:6; see also Psalm 148, Daniel 3:59–81). As the *Catechism* states, "By their mere existence they bless [God] and give him glory" (no. 2416). Second, through their lives and activities, animals serve God's plan. "Each creature," Francis states, "has its own purpose. None is superfluous" (*Laudato Si'*, §84). The "importance and meaning of each creature" is found "within the entirety of God's plan" (*Laudato Si'*, §86). Even the stones "cry out" to God (Luke 19:40). So, in their own distinctive way, animals do have acts that are directed toward God.

With these God-directed responses by animals in mind, we can return to our trinitarian framework and consider the possibility that the Spirit, who is co-Agent with the creature and Bond between the creature and God, embraces not only humans but also animals. The Spirit is immanent in all creation (the Spirit is sent forth to "renew the face of earth," Psalm 104:30), and thus can be both co-Agent in animal activity and Bond between animals and their God. The creature's capacity to praise God, just by being the creature it is, can become, through the co-labor of the Spirit, a form of obedience to the divine will. Thus, in a manner, animals *can* say "yes" to God, though in a different mode than a human person's "yes." This is a possibility that Thomas Aquinas recognized: "Even dumb animals are said to obey God, on account of the natural instinct whereby they are moved by God"; animals "partake of the Divine Reason by obeying it."[9]

I suggest, then, that in a trinitarian framework, all creatures, humans and nonhumans, are saved by Christ through the bond of the Spirit; this bond joins them to the God-human Jesus Christ and draws them into the eternal life of God. Both humans and nonhumans are active in this bond. For humans, it is a matter of freely assenting to God's offer. For animals, their assent is given just by being the creatures God made them to be. Theirs is not a free choice, but their active praise of God is still, nonetheless, a form of obedience to God. And this obediential praise of God is one that, we can hope, will be accepted by God and, through the bond of the Spirit, joined to the eternal praise of the saints.

We can't impose the same model of human salvation on animals. God works to save creatures according to the particular nature of each creature. Animals do not have the free choice that humans have, and so their salvation cannot take the same form as the salvation of humans. However, through the Spirit, they can still be integrated into Christ. Moreover, as we've noted, animals had no free choice in Adam's sin or in the suffering they've endured as a consequence of it. Humanity *freely* sinned, and, as a result, the natural world *unfreely* suffered. Perhaps, then, in Christ and through the Spirit, the solidarity between humanity and the rest of creation will begin a new phase that reverses the process, so that just as animals once, without choice, fell with humanity, so will they now, without choice, be raised with it.

THE CHURCH'S PRAYER FOR SALVATION: ANIMALS INCLUDED

I noted above humanity's role in mediating, with and through Christ, creation's salvation. Francis affirms the principle but modifies it with a surprising twist: "Human beings . . . are called *to lead all creatures back to their Creator*" (*Laudato Si'*, §83, emphasis added). In contrast to other church statements where humanity's role seems passive and creation is simply pulled along for a salvific ride (recall *Lumen Gentium*, §48: "The "entire world . . . attains to its end through [humanity]"), Francis implies that human persons are to have more of an active role in creation's salvation. What does he mean by this?

I confess, I'm not sure. However, one place where we do assist in the salvation of our human neighbors is through prayer, especially in the Eucharist. In the Eucharist, Catholics express in word and ritual their participation in Christ's life and death and prayerfully unite with him in his salvific labor. If it is the case that humanity has some sort of active role to play in the salvation of animals, we'd expect to find a confirmation of it in the Church's liturgy.

And we do, sort of. One of the Eucharistic Prayers (Eucharistic Prayer IV) explicitly mentions nonhuman creatures in a way that fits with an animal-inclusive theology of salvation. (The Eucharistic Prayer is the central prayer of the Mass. It begins with the Preface Dialogue ["The Lord be with you," "And with your spirit," . . .]; continues with the *Sanctus* ["Holy, Holy, Holy"]; and ends with the Great Amen immediately before the Our Father.) Since the Catholic tradition understands the Eucharistic celebration as the place where the work of Christ continues and where the people of God are drawn into that work, the inclusion of creatures in the Fourth Eucharistic Prayer is significant. In lifting up nonhuman creatures in the liturgy, the Church expresses in symbolic acts its hope that creation will be included, somehow, in Christ's gift and its belief that these prayerful rites can, through the bonding work of the Spirit, effect that inclusion.

We have seen that many early church theologians believed Christ's salvation has a cosmic scope. Some of them viewed the day when Christians gathered to worship as symbolic of this cosmic salvation. Since the first day of the Jewish week (Sunday in today's reckoning) was also the day of Christ's resurrection (Easter Sunday), it became the day of worship for the Christian community. Early Christians saw in the day a symbol of creation's renewal: Just as the former creation began on the first day of the week (Genesis 1), so also its renewal begins with the start of a new week (i.e., Easter Sunday).

The Church incorporated this belief in creation's renewal into the community's formal ritual and prayers (what became known as the Eucharist or, in more common language, the Mass). Irenaeus (d. 202), for example, associated the gifts of bread and wine with all of creation. And in offering the gifts of bread and wine to God, the liturgy effectively lifts up all creation to God and draws it into the Christian community's celebration of Christ's saving act.[10]

The Eucharistic Prayers of the Eastern Churches preserved this ritualized inclusion of creation's salvation in their Sunday worship. Until Vatican II, however, the Latin Rite of the Catholic Church scarcely referred to creation's salvation. That changed in the late 1960s, owing to the liturgical reforms of Vatican II. Additional prayers were added, including the Fourth Eucharistic Prayer. Reflecting its Eastern heritage and unique among the Eucharistic Prayers of the Roman Missal (of which there are now ten in the English translation), the prayer explicitly includes creation in its ritual movements and in its words of thanksgiving, sanctification, and eschatological hope. Though the prayer was new to the Catholic Church of the 1960s, parts of it go back to two ancient liturgies of the fourth century (the *Apostolic Constitutions* and the Liturgy of St. Basil).[11] The prayer therefore is another example of a practice that occurred during the time of Vatican II: the retrieval of earlier traditions in order to serve contemporary theological needs. In this case, the retrieval expanded options for the Church's formal prayer so that the Catholic community can now express its embrace of a cosmic eschatology at the Eucharist.

The Preface of Eucharistic Prayer IV opens with a proclamation of God's goodness to both humanity and creation and looks with expectation to the sanctification of both: "[You] have made all that is, so that you might fill your creatures with blessings and bring joy to many of them by the glory of your light." With the angels, the human community gives "voice to every creature under heaven." After the *Sanctus*, the prayer praises God for fashioning all creatures "in wisdom and in love." The work of Christ is then recounted and the theme of creation's sanctification more explicitly stated. Christ "proclaimed the good news of salvation" and sent the Holy Spirit so that "we might no longer live for ourselves" and that God "might sanctify creation to the full." After the words of institution, the celebrant offers up to God Christ's "Body and Blood . . . which brings salvation to the whole world." At its close, the prayer looks with hopeful anticipation of the kingdom that is to come: "There, with the whole of creation, freed from the corruption of sin and death, may we glorify you through Christ our Lord, through whom you bestow on the world all that is good."

The Fourth Eucharistic Prayer reflects the Church's commitment to a cosmic eschatology, that God's saving act in Christ is directed to all creation. Through the prayer, the cosmic Christ theme of summing up "all things" in Christ takes a eucharistic form. Creation is lifted up at Mass in the gifts of bread and wine, then transformed into Christ, his body and blood. In that transformation of the bread and wine, creation itself becomes united to Christ.

The idea that the Eucharist celebrates and effects the salvation of nonhuman creation finds support in papal writings after Vatican II. John Paul II writes that the Eucharist "unites heaven and earth" and "permeates all creation." Through its formal prayers, the Church celebrates that Christ "gives back to the Creator and Father all creation redeemed" (*Ecclesia de Eucharistia*, §8). Similarly, Benedict XVI states that in the Eucharist, "creation is projected towards divinization" and "toward unification with the Creator himself" ("Homily: Sacred Body and Blood of Christ," June 15, 2006). Christian worship, Benedict wrote before becoming pope, is the "soul of the covenant"; it "not only saves [humankind] but is also meant to draw the whole of reality into communion with God."[12] Pope Francis states the same: "The Eucharist joins heaven and earth; it embraces and penetrates all creation" (*LS*, §236). The Eucharist gives the Church's prayers for redemption a cosmic reach, extending it to all creation.

As is the case for the other creation-friendly texts we've examined, we should be cautious about reading too much into these regarding the question of whether specific animals of the present age will join us in heaven. Nonetheless, it is telling that the Church has expressed in liturgical form, in its central act of worship, a belief that all creation is to be saved, however vaguely that salvation is understood or presented.

Finally, I want to note briefly a different form of creaturely prayer: the blessing of animals, typically on the Feast of St. Francis of Assisi (October 4). The practice has a European precursor in the blessings of animals on the feast of St. Anthony the Abbot. But the custom in the United States, which has exploded in popularity over the last several decades, likely goes back to a 1985 service held on the Feast of St. Francis at the Episcopal Cathedral of St. John the Divine in Manhattan. The service drew a lot of media attention for the appearance of a throng of animals, domestic and wild, which were blessed at the altar.

The blessings are now widespread, offered in churches that span the ecumenical spectrum; their popularity is such that non-Christian venues have begun to host blessings on St. Francis's feast day. The blessings are driven as much by grassroots enthusiasm as they are local parish leadership, suggesting that changing Catholic attitudes toward animals is both a bottom-up phenomenon, encouraged by Catholics in the pew, and a top-down one, propelled by the Church's leadership.

We see the shift that's underway when we compare these local blessings to the official ones provided by the US Conference of Catholic Bishops (USCCB). The bishops' prayers appear in its 1989 *Book of Blessings,* a book that includes blessings for everything from churches and homes to fishing gear and gymnasiums. The prayers for animals found in the book only ask that God help animals to serve us well, not that he grant them health or happiness: "O God, . . . Reach out with your right hand and grant that these animals may serve our needs."[13] In contrast parish blessings typically attend to the interests of the animals themselves. One version states: "Lord God, maker of all living creatures. . . . You inspired St. Francis to call all of them his brothers and sisters. We ask you to bless this pet. By the power of your love, enable it to live according to your plan."[14] The prayer might not contain everything a pet caretaker would want; however, the blessing does have the virtue of acknowledging that animals might have some other purpose or interest besides that of serving humans.

We can attribute the differences between the two prayers partly to their different contexts. The bishops' prayer, written over thirty years ago, reflects a historical interest in blessing farm animals, while the parish blessing is typically directed to companion animals. Still, one could argue that insofar as the parish blessings reflect the spiritual interests of the Catholic faithful, both in terms of their content and popularity, they act as an unofficial signpost of the direction that the Spirit is leading the Church.

CONCLUSION

If animals are to be saved, it is because they have been included in the work of Christ. The Church has not embraced any particular theology of animal salvation, and so I have constructed one model for animal salvation. I do so to show that such a theology is possible using the resources of the Catholic theological tradition, not to present it as *the* correct model.

God saves, and his salvation need not be limited to humanity. During its long history, the Christian tradition has used various models for understanding how God effects salvation. They all center on the person of Jesus Christ and what God achieved through him in the events of the Easter Triduum—Holy Thursday, Good Friday, and Easter Sunday. I have approached this saving event through the lens of the trinitarian theology of Hans Urs von Balthasar, one of the most influential Catholic theologians of the twentieth century.

In God's triune life, the Father, the Son, and the Holy Spirit exist in a loving and eternal interchange. Balthasar's interpretation of this interchange underscores that it is dramatic, analogously speaking, in that it is always new and creative, not static. In the events of the Easter Triduum, God did something new. Jesus took on the weight of sin, and insofar as he represented sinful humanity, he endured humanity's alienation from God. The Father, however, embraced his Son, raising him up in the resurrection, and in so doing, embraced all of humanity with him. Humanity is thus saved through the death and resurrection of Jesus Christ because we are now drawn into the acting "space" of the Son, turned to the Father in the eternal bond of the Holy Spirit.

Balthasar's metaphor of a capacious acting space between the Father and the Son, absolutely united in the Spirit, offers a way for us to imagine God's restoration of his relationship with humanity. The space within the triune life, whose vibrant and dramatic contours are fundamentally shaped by the eternal giving-and-receiving exchange among the divine Persons, has, through the events of Christ's cross and resurrection, expanded to include the human person.

Balthasar's model can be adapted to include nonhuman creatures. The Spirit's mission to liquefy Christ is key to this. The Spirit stamps Christ on all of creation by establishing a bond between the Godhead and all God's creatures, both human and nonhuman.

Against the argument that animals do not have the freedom necessary for accepting God's offer, I suggest two things: (1) Theological models that are appropriate for understanding human salvation cannot be simply transposed, without any adaptation, to animals; and (2) animals have been given a type of agency, a capacity to act, that God can use to draw them to himself.

In their praise of God, just by being what they are, animals are already saying "yes" to God. So, against the view that animals are incapable of accepting God's offer, I argue that God has given animals their own way of responding to his call.

These musings are a way to understand how God has achieved the final liberation of nonhuman animals. But creation's movement toward its union with God has already begun in the present age. In the central act of the Catholic faith, the Eucharist, the Church both celebrates what Christ has achieved, for humanity and creation, and effects it, expanding the work of the historical person Jesus Christ in order that it continues in the present age. It is appropriate then that recent popes, following early Church thinkers, have seen the Eucharist as a place where creation is, through word and symbol, lifted up to God and saved. In the Eucharist, to repeat Pope Benedict's words, "creation is projected towards divinization."

NOTES

1. "God is perfectly personal and relational, and since we are created in the image of God . . . we will be most like God when we live" in a way that "conforms to who God is." Catherine Mowry LaCugna, "The Practical Trinity," *The Christian Century* 109, no. 22 (1992), 678–82 at 682.
2. Balthasar develops his dramatic, trinitarian theology in *Theo-Drama: Theological Dramatic Theory,* 5 volumes, trans. Graham Harrison (San Francisco: Ignatius Press, 1988–1998). For a quick overview, see Declan Marmion and Rik van Nieuwenhove, *An Introduction to the Trinity* (Cambridge: Cambridge University Press, 2010), 176–85.
3. A brief discussion of Balthasar's arguments for animal salvation can be found in Todd Walatka, *Von Balthasar and the Option for the Poor: Theodramatics in the Light of Liberation Theology* (Washington, DC: Catholic University of America Press, 2017), 49–51.
4. For more on these issues, see Frederick C. Bauerschmidt and James J. Buckley, *Catholic Theology: An Introduction* (Chichester, UK: Wiley-Blackwell, 2016), 28–65.
5. Thomas Hughson, "Interpreting Vatican II: 'A New Pentecost,'" *Theological Studies* 69, no. 1 (2008): 3–37.
6. Hans Urs von Balthasar, "The Holy Spirit as Love," in *Explorations in Theology*, vol. 3, *Creator Spirit*, trans. Brian McNeil (San Francisco: Ignatius Press, 1993), 117–34.
7. Walter Kasper, *The God of Jesus Christ* (New York: Crossroad, 1994), 198–231.
8. Elizabeth Johnson also argues for a trinitarian redemption of the cosmos through an appeal to Christ's "deep Incarnation." Elizabeth A. Johnson, *Ask the Beasts: Darwin and the God of Love* (London: Bloomsbury, 2014), 192–200.
9. Aquinas, *Summa Theologiae*, II-II.83.10, *ad.* 3; and I-II.93.5, *ad.* 2.
10. Irenaeus, *Against Heresies*, book IV, chapter 17.5 and book IV, chapter 18.5; both are available on the New Advent website, https://www.newadvent.org/fathers/0103.htm.
11. For more on these ancient prayers, see Ronald C. D. Jasper and G. J. Cuming, *Prayers of the Eucharist: Early and Reformed*, 3rd ed. (Collegeville, MN: Liturgical Press, 1990).

12. Joseph Ratzinger, *Spirit of the Liturgy* (San Francisco: Ignatius Press, 2000), 27.
13. United States Conference of Catholic Bishops, *Book of Blessings* (Collegeville, MN: Liturgical Press, 1989), 415.
14. Kevin Mackin, "Blessing of Animals," *St. Anthony Messenger*, October 2019, https://www.franciscanmedia.org/st-anthony-messenger/blessing-of-animals/.

FURTHER READING

Most of the sources for this chapter's discussions can be found in chapter 4 of *All God's Animals: A Catholic Theological Framework for Animal Ethics*. Washington, DC: Georgetown University Press, 2019, 133–70.

Church Documents

The most significant Catholic Church documents are available on the Vatican website, www.vatican.va.

Documents from the Second Vatican Council can be found here: https://www.vatican.va/archive/hist_councils/ii_vatican_council/index.htm.

The Vatican's website has a portal for each pope where their writings, homilies, audiences, and public statements can be found: https://www.vatican.va/holy_father/index.htm.

The Theology of Hans Urs von Baltharsar

Balthasar's theology is difficult. Aiden Nichols provides a guide to his trilogy:

Nichols, Aiden. *The Word Has Been Abroad: A Guide through Balthasar's Aesthetics*. Washington, DC: Catholic University of America Press, 1998.

Nichols, Aiden. *No Bloodless Myth: A Guide through Balthasar's Dramatics*. Washington, DC: Catholic University of America Press, 2000.

Nichols, Aiden. *Say It Is Pentecost: A Guide through Balthasar's Logic*. Washington, DC: Catholic University of America Press, 2001.

Other Theologies of Creation's Salvation

Edwards, Denis. *Partaking of God: Trinity, Evolution, and Ecology*. Collegeville, MN: Liturgical Press, 2014.

Johnson, Elizabeth. *Creation and the Cross: The Mercy of God for a Planet in Peril*. Maryknoll, NY: Orbis, 2018.

Middleton, Richard. *A New Heaven and a New Earth: Reclaiming Biblical Eschatology*. Grand Rapids: Baker Academic, 2014.

The Eucharist

Jasper, Ronald Claud Dudley, and G. J. Cuming. *Prayers of the Eucharist: Early and Reformed.* Fourth edition. Edited by Paul F. Bradshaw and Maxwell E. Johnson. Collegeville, MN: Liturgical Press, 1990.

LaVerdiere, Eugene. *The Eucharist in the New Testament and the Early Church.* Collegeville, MN: Liturgical Press, 1996.

CHAPTER 6

Animals in Heaven

On the sparsely populated island of Torcello, near Venice, stands the Cathedral of Santa Maria Assunta. The church was founded in 639, but most of the present structure dates back to the eleventh century. On the west wall of the structure is a stunning, twelfth-century mosaic of the Last Judgment. One of the scenes depicts angels blowing trumpets to wake the dead for their resurrection. Rising up with those resurrecting humans are birds, beasts, and fish. These animals are needed, in the mind of the artist, so that they can return the parts of humans they had eaten during their earthly lives. Thus one side of the mosaic shows beasts and birds regurgitating body parts and sometimes whole humans, while the other side shows fish and sea monsters doing the same. Presumably these parts would soon be reassembled to complete the resurrection of the dead.[1]

We might wonder about the theology underlying the mosaic's depiction of the resurrection, but it is right on one count: Christianity takes seriously its belief that our lives in heaven will be embodied ones. Jesus revealed as much. The disciples saw and interacted with the *physical*, resurrected Christ. They even ate fish with him (Luke 24:41–43; John 21:9–13).

Complementing this stress on bodily life, and sometimes seen as in tension with it, is the emphasis that Catholicism has placed on the spiritual contemplation that will shape our heavenly lives: the beatific vision. In it, we will behold God, lovingly, intimately, and personally, in a spiritual encounter that will fulfill all human longings. Given the centrality of this spiritual vision in the Catholic understanding of heaven, any portrayal of animals in heaven should be able to take account of it while preserving Catholic belief in the bodiliness of life in heaven. Making sense of that possibility is the task of this chapter.

NATURE AND GRACE

My first step in constructing a theory regarding animals in heaven is to note a Catholic commitment that informs its understanding of life in heaven: the distinction it makes between nature and grace.[2] The commitment has both shaped and constrained Catholicism's view by encouraging a middle position in regard to humanity's final transformation: We will be neither the same (because grace will change us) nor unrecognizably different (our nature will endure). My approach to animals in heaven is likewise guided by this commitment.

Human Nature: Healed and Elevated

In a Catholic understanding of God's creation, all creatures have a "nature," something that marks them to be the particular type of creature they are—for example, the particular abilities they have and what constitutes their flourishing and happiness. Humans have a nature, as do dogs, bees, and octopuses. Members of each species have characteristic ways of being that are recognizable to us. So when I refer to a creature's nature in this context, this is what I mean: not nature in the sense of the great outdoors but nature in the sense of those characteristic qualities or ways of being that we associate with a particular type of creature. Again, humans have their nature, but so do cheetahs, trees, flowers, roaches, and so forth.

Catholic thought holds that God preserves the nature of each creature even after the Fall. The Fall harms humanity, but it does not destroy its fundamental nature. Likewise God will also preserve human nature in the life to come: It will not be radically changed from what it is now. Thus, for example, we will not become bodiless spirits (e.g., angels) but will remain bodily beings.

God likewise preserves the natures of other creatures after the Fall (e.g., the respective natures of the elephant, the mouse, and the lilac). Animals were changed by the Fall, but they still remained, at some fundamental level, the sort of creatures they were in paradise. As is the case for humans, God did not allow the Fall to radically subvert the respective natures shared by members of each species. Similarly, if animals go to heaven, they will presumably still be the type of creatures they are now.

The point in all this is to highlight a principle that has been important for Catholicism: God preserves the integrity of what God creates. Each person, each species, has an original goodness that God always protects and that no amount of evildoing can obliterate. God desired the goodness of what he created, and because God continues to cherish that goodness, he will not change humans into a different type of being once they get to heaven.

That's the "nature" side of the nature and grace distinction. What about grace? In everyday theological parlance, grace is a gift from God, a blessing that is unmerited. This can take the form of moral assistance—for example, grace helps us act generously and wisely and overcome sinful habits and inclinations. For such activities, grace assists our nature to perform as it should. Humans were made to be good: to act justly and live in praise of God. Ideally we could do that without a special intervention by God. However, because of the Fall, we now find it difficult to be true to our human natures and be the kind of persons God intended us to be. Grace then helps by *healing* us, making it possible for us to recover our natural ability to be good.

This understanding of grace is shared by many Christian traditions. In addition, however, the Catholic tradition holds that grace also *elevates* the human person, so that we can act in ways that exceed what is natural to us. God not only saves us from the consequences of sin (i.e., grace *heals* us) but goes one step further. Through the free gift made possible in Christ's life, death, and resurrection, we are drawn into an intimate *friendship* with God. In our natural capacity as humans, we are not able to have such an intimate relationship with God, but through grace we are. This friendship will reach its perfection in the age to come. Thus in heaven human nature will be elevated—different from what it was in paradise but not fundamentally so.

In sum, nature is basically the totality of those fundamental qualities that each of us shares as human persons, identifying us as human and not something else. When God bestows grace on us, we are both healed of the wounds of sin and also elevated to a new destiny. Whatever we will be in the future world, in heaven, we will still be human, transformed through grace but human nonetheless. Thus the Catholic distinction between nature and grace—or between healed human nature and elevated human nature—highlights that we do not cease being human because of grace.

Animals and the Distinction between Nature and Grace

What does this have to do with animals? I have already noted one aspect of the nature/grace distinction as it applies to animals: If animals are in heaven, their natures, it would seem, will be preserved. Animals will still be the type of creatures that God created them to be. Cats will still be cats, and dogs will still be dogs. As with humans, God preserves the natures of the creatures he creates.

In healing animals (healing their natures), grace returns them to the form that God intended them to be before the wounds of sin harmed them. As imagined in Genesis, animals in paradise were peaceful, lived in harmony with other creatures, and were obedient to humanity's compassionate governance. Correspondingly, such is the state to which God's healing grace will return them in the age to come. With their natures healed, animals will live free of violence, disease, and death.

That's the "healing" part of grace's operation. The question for us is whether God might do something more in the lives of animals, something analogous to how grace elevates humans to a new relationship with God. As I've noted, Scripture and church teachings are mostly silent regarding what, concretely, it will mean for God to save an animal. We just do not "know how all things will be transformed" (John Paul II, "Audience," May 14, 1986). Nonetheless one possible understanding of animals being elevated by grace is to imagine that God draws animals into a new relationship with him, one not possible based simply on the animal's nature. Though the character of this relationship would vary according to the capacities of the particular animal, in every case it will be life-giving for the animal. Grace heals and elevates—humans and animals. And as is the case for humans, this elevation will not radically alter the type of creature they are, assuming that God wills to preserve the nature of the animals he created. Giraffes will not develop a hive mind, and beavers will not start discussing theoretical physics as part of their play.

CRITIQUES OF ANIMALS IN HEAVEN

Before turning to the main task at hand, to sketch a heaven for animals, I want to address some of the "nonsensical" arguments that I criticized in passing in the last chapter. These arguments try to show that the idea of animals in heaven leads to some sort of absurdity. Since these arguments have some traction in the Catholic blogosphere, it would be good to take a moment to note them.

Among the more lighthearted arguments is the concern that heaven would be too crowded if God allowed animals to join us. Given that there are up to 2 trillion galaxies in the observable universe and on average each of these contain 100 million stars, we can assume that God is up to the task. Still, the argument raises an interesting challenge: If heaven is going to be some kind of communion, isn't it a stretch to imagine that we will be in a genuine relationship with all these creatures? The short of it is, yes. However, the problem does not disappear even if we keep heaven as an exclusively human club. According to some estimates, more than 100 billion humans have lived and died on earth since the species first arose 100,000 years ago, and therefore our social networking capacities will be overwhelmed regardless.

A possible response would be to recall that Christ is the center of all things, the one in whom all things will be restored. We can imagine that he will act as the mediator of our experiences with all other creatures and that through him we will be in communion with them. This doesn't eliminate the challenge, but it shifts the explanatory burden to the mystery of the God-human and the transformation he effects in us.

Another complaint, also lighthearted, argues that expanding the scope of heaven would have us live for all eternity in a realm filled with unpleasant creatures—ants, tapeworms, *Staphylococcus* bacteria, and roaches. Against this ugly creature scenario, we can imagine that just as all creatures will be transformed in the age to come, so also will our attitudes toward them. If God enjoys receiving the praises of these creatures in this life and wants their praise to continue in the next, then we will join God in that future age and also take joy in them.

A different response, however, would be to build on what I suggested in the last chapter: The form that a particular animal's salvation takes could vary according to the particular capacities of each animal. Salvation for amoebas and bacteria would be different from that of a dog; God might decide to save them in a way that does not involve restoring each and every one of them.

A more respectable critique begins with the view that heaven is a reward for those who have earned it. Since animals can't be "good," they don't deserve the reward. In the last chapter I criticized a version of this argument: Animals can't freely choose God. Against that, I maintained that the theological model for human salvation does not necessarily work for animals.

However, on two other counts we can challenge this animals-lack-merit argument. First, the idea that heaven is a reward for anyone is problematic. Yes, the formal prayers of the Church do regularly use language of merit and reward. For example, in the Second Eucharistic Prayer, the Church asks God that "we may *merit* to be co-heirs to eternal life." But the idea that any of us deserves heaven must be countered with the more fundamental belief that all credit for our achieved goodness lies with God. As Augustine put it, "God does not crown [reward] your merits as your merits, but as His own gifts."[3]

Second, the Church already hopes that at least some of God's human creatures (for example, unbaptized babies) who have not had a chance either to participate in the sacraments or respond freely to God will still go to heaven. Thus a 2007 International Theological Commission (ITC) document approved by Pope Benedict sidelined the notion of Limbo, the place where innocent, unbaptized babies were supposed to go. The conclusion of the commission is hopeful: "The many factors that we have considered above give serious theological and liturgical grounds for hope that unbaptised infants who die will be saved and enjoy the Beatific Vision" (International Theological Commission, "Un-Baptised Infants," April 19, 2007).

The most serious obstacle to imagining animals in heaven for many Catholics is that the beatific vision—a spiritual, contemplative knowing of God—is beyond the capacity of nonhuman creatures. If animals cannot share in the beatific vision, it is argued, they don't belong in heaven.

It is impossible to disregard the beatific vision in any account of heavenly life given the significant theological and dogmatic weight it has in the Catholic tradition. In a papal bull in 1336, Pope Benedict XII defined the beatific vision as dogma. He described it as seeing "the divine essence [of God] with an intuitive vision . . . without the mediation of any creature." The justification for the belief is provided by biblical texts such as 1 John 3:2, where the author states that in the age to come, "we shall be like [God], for we shall see him as he is" (see also Matthew 5:8: "Blessed are the clean of heart, for they will see God"). Since it is not possible for animals to have an unmediated vision of God—one that does not rely on the physical senses like eyes and ears but on a spiritual and intellectual cognition made possible by grace—they are not able to be in heaven, or so the argument goes.

Against this view, we first recall that life in heaven will be a genuinely embodied one. We will not be just spirits contemplating God but spiritual creatures with active, perceptive bodies. The bodily nature of our heavenly existence presumably means that we will continue to enjoy corporeal experiences, however transformed they may be—physical experiences like seeing, hearing, touching, smelling, and tasting. This enduring physicality of heavenly life has the secondary effect of opening heaven's door to animals. Since animals experience bodily joys, they can still enjoy heaven, even if they do not have the capacity to contemplate God spiritually.

In its description of heaven, the *Catechism of the Catholic Church* takes account of both its spiritual (the beatific vision) *and* its bodily dimensions.[4] The description shifts slightly as the *Catechism* moves through the events of the end times, as it must. In Catholic teaching we are not rejoined with our resurrected bodies immediately upon death but must wait until the final age when Christ returns in the Second Coming. Thus the *Catechism*'s account of heaven is careful to attend to differences in our experiences of the two stages—the interim period that begins with each person's death (but before they are rejoined with their bodies) and the final, everlasting period ushered in by Jesus's Second Coming and our bodily resurrection.

During the interim period, each person receives a "particular judgment" upon his or her death regarding the fundamental orientation of their lives—heaven or purgatory for those who have accepted God's offer and eternal damnation for those who have refused it (*Catechism,* no. 1021). Those who are judged to be among the blessed will begin partaking of the beatific vision either immediately after death or after a time of purgation. The *Catechism* describes this bodiless state in nos. 1023–1028. We will see God "face to face" (*Catechism,* no. 1023) and contemplate "God in his heavenly glory" (*Catechism,* no. 1028). Heaven is the "perfect life with the Most Holy Trinity" and a communion "of life and love with the Trinity, with the Virgin Mary, the angels and all the blessed" (*Catechism,* no. 1024).

In the section titled "The Hope of the New Heaven and the New Earth" (nos. 1042–1050), the *Catechism* turns to the final age. This final age occurs after the Second Coming of Christ, the Last Judgment, and our bodily resurrection. Because the saints are now living an embodied life in heaven, the language used here to describe this state is, correspondingly, more explicitly creation-inclusive. We're told that at this time we will see the full coming of the kingdom of God, which was inaugurated in Christ and will include not only the liberation of humanity but that of the cosmos itself: "At the end of time, the Kingdom of God will come in its fullness. . . . The universe itself will be renewed" (*Catechism,* no. 1042). Reflecting the "cosmic Christ" theme that appears in Ephesians and Colossians, the text states that heaven will be the "definitive realization of God's plan to bring under a single head all things in [Christ], things in heaven and things on earth" (*Catechism,* no. 1043).

For humanity, heaven will be "the community of the redeemed," no longer wounded in any way but sharing in "the beatific vision . . . [which] will be the ever-flowing well-spring of happiness, peace, and mutual communion" (*Catechism,* no. 1045). The *Catechism* states, citing the Romans 8 passage we studied in chapter 3, that nonhuman creation will also be "set free from its bondage to decay" and transformed so as to share in humanity's "glorification in the risen Jesus Christ" (*Catechism,* nos. 1046–1047).

Though the section states that this final incorporation of "all things in Christ" will include nonhuman creation, it is, unsurprisingly, clearer in its description of humanity's incorporation than that of nonhuman creatures.

Thus the section adds—citing Vatican II's *Gaudium et Spes* (§39) and in keeping with the Church's reticence regarding animals in the next life—that we do not know "the way in which the universe will be transformed" (*Catechism*, no. 1048).

Still, though cryptic, these statements affirm that nonhuman creatures will in some form join us in heaven. Moreover the reason for their presence is precisely because of their relationship with Christ—that is, they are brought "under" Christ's head and share in humanity's glorification "in" Christ. Thus we have good reason to resist the humans-only argument based on the beatific vision. With the resurrection of the dead, life in heaven will be a bodily one and tied to the risen, bodily Christ. It follows that heaven can include animals that are, as traditionally understood, merely bodily creatures.

ANIMALS IN HEAVEN: A SKETCH

The final task left to us in developing our case for animals in heaven is to show, against critics, that the idea does make sense. Even more so than any other argument, this one will be speculative and figurative. We know that life in heaven will exceed anything we can anticipate in the present, so any musings will not be adequate to the reality. Even the central image that the Catholic tradition has used to depict the next life, the beatific vision, points to an experience that inherently exceeds the power of imagination.

Nonetheless creative, figurative depictions of heaven and the journey to it—Dante's *Paradiso*, John Bunyan's *Pilgrim's Progress*, C. S. Lewis's *The Great Divorce* and *The Last Battle*—have an established place in Christian literature not only because of their innate literary merit but also because they help us understand, through symbolic and poetic language, our hoped-for future. These depictions shape our passions, stirring in us the moral energy necessary to live generously in the present with an eye to that future. I have no intent, of course, of trying my own hand at a literary interpretation. My main goal is only to sketch a version of what that life may be in order to defend the idea that God intends to include animals in it.

We have already identified images and themes that provide the basic contours of a heavenly life inclusive of animals: God's desire for a covenantal relationship with each and every creature, God's final plan to sum up all things in Christ (the cosmic Christ theme), a new creation idealized in the peaceable kingdom of Isaiah 11, and the enduring bodiliness of heavenly life.

Our imagination is further guided by the Catholic principle we examined above: Grace heals and elevates nature; it does not replace the individual natures of animals with radically different ones. We will continue to be humans in the next life, and, we can suppose, dogs will still be dogs and cats will still be cats. In that vein, Vatican II speaks of the present world as a "foreshadowing" of the world to come (*Gaudium et Spes*, §39). Though "the visible universe . . . is destined to be transformed" (*Catechism*, no. 1047)—"resplendently transfigured," to use Pope Francis's phrase—it will still preserve the natures of the individual creatures who have been part of this world. We can speak then of "transfigured natures" in which the natures of animals continue to exist in the world to come—transformed in unimaginable ways and yet in continuity with their natures in the present age.[5]

So what might such transfigured natures look like in regard to animals? Based on Jewish and Christian imagery found in the Bible, we can say that the future world will be liberated from any violence and suffering—as the passage from Romans puts it, it will be "set free from slavery to corruption." Correlatively we can assume that life for animals in the world to come will reflect the ideals of the kingdom: harmony, joy, and unending life.

We also know that God created the world so that it would reflect his triune life, and thus we can expect that heaven's creatures will also be bonded together through relationships and ultimately the covenant with God. Given the importance of this and God's goal to "sum up" all things in Christ, it makes sense to believe that animals will share, in some form, a relationship with God in Jesus Christ. We laid the foundation for this in the last chapter with our discussion of the Holy Spirit as the divine bond with all creation.

We can take this one step further: In light of the Catholic idea of grace as elevating, perhaps animals too will be elevated so that they can, like humans, become companions of God, in whatever manner such a relationship is possible for them as the animals they are. God has blessed individual animals with relational capacities that are characteristic of their species. They express these capacities in relationships with their conspecifics (fellow species members) and with animals from other species. We can imagine then that God can, should God will to do so, augment and heighten those capacities by establishing a new relationship with animals.

For some animals, this new relationship with God might merely be a primitive awareness of a comforting presence or an instinctual confidence that all will be well; they have been freed from apprehension and fear. Other animals might become more explicitly aware of God's presence as an encouraging and even personal background to their thoughts. Or perhaps God will become an unnamed "partner" that shares in the animal's life and play. Some animals might have the cognitive apparatus to experience this partner as a specific bodily person (the resurrected Christ) and perhaps even know the name of this companion as "Jesus"—the beloved whom they've encountered and have come to enjoy. My point is that even if it is the case that only the human person can be elevated to the state of intimate friendship with God, that does not exclude the possibility that God can have other forms of relationships, as appropriate, with animals.[6]

My sketch of a heaven for animals so far is guided by a Catholic instinct that the natures of creatures are both preserved and transfigured. This instinct, however, confronts a challenge that I glossed over above but merits further consideration: Does the preservation of an animal's nature require that predator animals continue to be violent predators in the eschaton? The category of predatory creatures comprises a diverse range of animals. Beyond the familiar apex predators (e.g., lions, tigers, and bears), it includes creatures less threatening to humans like sparrows, cats, and seals. Creation in the eschaton would be impoverished by the absence of such a variety of creatures.

With many theologians, I believe that violence will have no place in the world to come. Therefore *if* it is the case that the *essential* property defining the nature of a particular animal is its violent predation, then it does not seem possible for it to be in heaven—at least, not without it becoming an entirely different animal. Put in biblical terms, Can an animal still be called a wolf if it is "a guest of the lamb" or called a leopard if it "lie[s] down with the young goat" or a lion if it "browse[s]" with a calf (Isaiah 11:6)? Isn't something essential about their identity lost if they cease their predation and become gentle companions with other animals?

I do not believe that the manner in which a species obtains its nutrition is an essential, defining property of that species. Support for that can be found in the figurative depiction of animals in Genesis 1. But more importantly, all predatory animals have defining characteristics *in addition to* that of predation that mark them as members of a particular species. Besides their distinctive mannerisms in the way they move and rest, species also recreate in distinctive ways. Bears like to play with supple trees that they can bend and then climb on. Otters take advantage of slippery slopes as make-do slides. Dolphins blow bubble rings, which they then swim through.

In addition, species are distinctive in the ways they socialize with conspecifics. We saw an example of this in chapter 2 when discussing the social arrangements of elephants. Other species likewise have their own peculiar characteristics. Pods of whales sing distinctive songs that are sometimes changed by an "influencer" within the pod. Crows live in family groups typically composed of two parents and their offspring from the present year and the previous ones, with the older chicks helping to raise the younger ones. Monkeys are known for their strong friendships and spend hours in ritual grooming as a way of cementing social bonds. Starlings join together in numbers exceeding 500 to perform their stunning, mesmerizing murmuration until a handful of leaders decide it is time to roost. "Each bird seems to be in tune with some mysterious choreography, so that the flock wheels, dives, and climbs as one, pulsing with kinetic energy."[7] Octopuses are typically solitary creatures, but few mothers in the animal world are as self-sacrificing for their children as they.

That predators develop friendships among themselves is particularly telling. It shows that predators already, in the present age, have the capacity for relationships that fit the harmonious ideals of the kingdom. In chapter 2, we noted some of these friendships in predator species—for example, chimpanzees, whales, badgers, coyotes, lions, and penguins. These relationships are not extraordinary occurrences but a characteristic way in which some species interact with special conspecifics. Moreover, such nonpredatory behavior increases if the predator is not in need of food or freed from the need to hunt for it.

Also interesting for us are the companionships that have been observed spanning different species. Some scientists believe that these unusual cross-species bonds show that companionship is vital to many species. Indeed, some bonds are not only cross-species but also straddle the predator/prey divide. Lionesses in the wild, for example, have adopted calves from their prey species, including oryx, springbok, and gazelles.[8] Most known cases of these predator/prey friendships, however, occur in zoos. One famous example transpired in a Russian safari park. As was the park's practice, a live goat was placed as food in the enclosure of Amur, a Siberian tiger. Instead of eating him, as he had done with previous goats, Amur became friends with the goat, named Timur. At least for a few months. Amur got frustrated with Timur's antics, and eventually the two had to be separated.[9]

One could argue, given the oddity of these interspecies relationships, that they hardly express characteristic behaviors. Perhaps so. But though abnormal, they show the possibility of a different way for that species to interact. If predator animals can develop, already in this present age, friendships with animals from other species, then their natures need not undergo a radical transformation in the resurrection; the foundation for a peaceable harmony with other animals is already part of what or who they are, if not always in reality, at least in potentiality. The animals can interact with each other in ways other than that of predation, and they do so without losing their identities as members of a particular species.

Thus, these distinctive, nonpredatory behaviors of species in the present age—socializing, forming friendships, playing in particular ways, and expressing characteristic mannerisms—justify a hope that the distinctive nature of a particular predatory species can be preserved in heaven without also including its present disposition toward violence. Lions can still be lions even if they cease being violent predators because other qualities define what it means to be a lion besides that of predation.

There is another way of addressing the issue: imagining that the predator/prey relationship is transformed into one of play. Instead of violent hunting (or fleeing from that violence), the interaction between the two former enemies becomes one of sports-like play where the predator pretends to hunt the prey while the prey playfully flees. Anyone watching dogs play has seen versions of this in their chasing, barking, play-biting, swiping, and lunging at each other; they joyfully pretend to fight without inflicting any violence on their playmates. Though the ecosystems of the present age require predation in order to keep them well-functioning, the forces leading to that requirement—the need for nutrition and the risk of overpopulation should the weak not be culled—will not exist in heaven. It is possible then that animals in heaven will still interact, but now transformed into a type of eternal, life-giving, and competitive play.

We have intimations of such play in our own recreational activities. Most of us have experienced acts that on one level are self-sacrificing but not ultimately so, being neither personally harmful nor destructive but life-giving: the delight in having a beloved child beat us at a game, the joy of sports among friends even in defeat, the communal delight of a game of charades even in loss, or—to include a cross-species example—playing tug of war with one's dog. These are all instances of competitive play where the experience of conquest or defeat matters less than the joy of seeing the other happy and the delight in being with companions in competitive play. These examples show the possibility of a transformed predation in which the drama of competitive play between predator and prey is experienced as joyful, life-giving, and self-realizing. My suggestion then is that the predator/prey tragedy can be transformed, not simply annulled, in heaven.

James Dickey famously describes one version of a transformed, heavenly ecosystem in his poem "The Heaven of Animals."[10] He portrays a new creation where plants are "outdoing" themselves. Animals in that age continue to be what they were in the present: "If they have lived in a wood / It is a wood." The predators have been transformed into the best version of themselves ("with claws and teeth grown perfect"). They attack prey as they have in this life, but the hunted animals "feel no fear" of them. And once killed by the predator, "[The prey] rise, they walk again."

I believe Dickey goes too far in including the destruction of creatures, even if temporary, as part of the eschaton. Still, his depiction offers one way of imagining the possibility that once pain, violence, and destruction are removed, the predator/prey dynamic could become a part of the peaceable and playful kingdom of God. What makes this depiction of animals in heaven particularly noteworthy is that it is not only the animal itself that is preserved and transfigured in the age to come. In Dickey's imaginings, what is preserved and transfigured about these animals is *both* the individual animals *and* their relationships with other animals. Thus not only are the lion's and gazelle's respective natures preserved and transfigured but so also is their relationship with each other.

Based on this, it seems possible to imagine that this transformation of relationships, in God's final liberation of the world, will extend to the entire field of interactions among creatures that compose an ecosystem. Understanding a heaven for animals in these terms—as both the salvation of individual animals and a holistic transformation of the entire natural order in all its interrelatedness—aligns well with the cosmic Christ theme (summing up all things in Christ) and the Church's emphasis on the interconnectedness of all creatures: "God wills the interdependence of creatures. . . . Creatures exist only in dependence on each other, to complete each other, in the service of each other" (*Catechism*, no. 340). God created a wondrous world whose creatures are interdependent in myriad ways, and we can imagine that God will still desire such a complex, interrelated world in the age to come.

This view of earth's final renewal addresses the aesthetic complaint raised by some. They argue that the transformation of all animals into merely peaceable creatures would diminish the grandeur and wonder of the natural world. Instead, in line with Dickey's poem, we can imagine a world where prey like rabbits and deer retain their gentle and timid species personalities and predators like cheetahs and sharks retain their aggressive and bold dispositions without compromising on the commitment to heaven as a place of joy and harmony.

And we don't need to wait till the eschaton to witness such play. In responding to the boredom often endured by wild animals in captivity, zoos have developed species-specific games for the animals that allow them to act as they would in the wild, though without any violence to another creature.[11] One Seattle zookeeper caring for a leopard, for example, plays a game of stalking with it, pretending that she doesn't see the leopard as it creeps up on her and then pounces (playfully). Even more delightful is a case at the San Diego Zoo where a wolf and two goats became close friends.

> When let outside, they will meet on opposite sides of the fence that separates their exhibits. Then the animals will begin racing back-and-forth along the fence, the goats jumping and bouncing up and down as though in the middle of a run for their lives. Before or afterwards, to show his friendly intent, the wolf tries to lick the goats faces. Having noticed how much the animals enjoy playing together, the keepers now bring them out at the same time. . . . [A]t the end of the day, the wolf will balk at going back into his cage until he sees that his friends [the goats] are safely locked up for the night.[12]

The reason for the behavioral change is not entirely the boredom of life in a zoo. Scientific evidence suggests that once the needs for food and security lessen, animals will occupy their days with behaviors that might seem purposeless to us but are quite entertaining for them. And sometimes this play will stretch to other species. In fact, "some researchers have made the case that predator and prey, stripped of the rules of the natural world, are actually well situated for friendship."[13] If such friendships were to be part of heaven, we could find predators and prey interacting and forming bonds of social interchange in ways that continue their characteristic natures in the present age, albeit without the violence. Each animal would act according to its species identity. Each would enjoy heaven's eternally interactive games without fear or pain, giving God glory through the drama of that animal's renewed life.

As sketched here, a heaven of animals is one in which animals will be transformed and yet still be the kind of creatures they presently are. They will all be in communion with God in Jesus Christ, in whatever manner and to whatever degree their transformed capacities allow. For some, it will be merely an instinctual knowledge that all is well, while for others, it will involve an encounter with a special human that the animal joyfully loves above all others and feels deeply loved in return. For all animals, they will know only the joy of an eternal play undertaken in ways characteristic of each animal species. In this new age, lions will enjoy the hunt nonviolently, and gazelles will enjoy escaping them or, perhaps, letting their lion companions catch them.

Even better, the renewed creation might be composed not only of the species and ecosystems of our own twenty-first century but also all those that have appeared in earth's history and will appear in its future. It would be a glorious world indeed: a world filled with a virtually infinite number of interlinked ecosystems—a *Jurassic Park*–esque domain of dinosaurs, a rainforest of brightly colored parrots and playful monkeys, an Australian coral reef filled with aquatic life, and a domestic sphere of cows, pigs, and beloved dogs and cats, all partaking in an eternal play according to the "rules" of each animal's identity. It would be quite a sight to enjoy with God for all eternity and a fitting praise for the relational God who created them.

I underscore, again, that my intent is not to argue for a particular depiction of animals in heaven. I am confident that the above depiction will be proven wrong on many counts, if for no other reason than we don't know how time or space will work or what our new bodies will be like. But more important than any other reason for the inadequacy is that God's plan will exceed in goodness and wonder whatever I or anyone else can imagine. My intent is only to argue, against critics, that we *can* imagine some sort of creaturely heaven, and thus the idea that animals will join us in heaven is not nonsensical.

CONCLUSION

The ultimate criterion for whether or not animals will be in heaven is not that it makes sense to us but that God desires it. Nonetheless it strengthens the case for animals in heaven if the prospect of their presence makes sense from a merely mortal vantage and is in keeping with Christian and Catholic principles. My discussion of how to imagine a transformed continuity between the animals of the present age and the new forms they might take in heaven is based on Christian norms and what seems reasonable from a human perspective. It is a speculative account that will be proven woefully inadequate in the eschaton. Even knowing that, I've forged ahead in order to counter Catholic voices, both contemporary and historical, that view the idea of animals in heaven as absurd.

But I believe this speculative project is warranted for another reason. The prospect that animals will be given another chapter to their stories is a cause for hope for everyone who is troubled by the suffering of animals in the present age. To encourage such hope, we must articulate it. And that means we must develop depictions, always inadequate, of that future age. Thus imaginative scenarios like the above have a motivational function, to empower our pilgrim journey by giving flesh to its destination.

Inadequate attempts, however, to depict that future age shouldn't so muddle the issue as to make the presence of animals in heaven depend on the success of our imagination. The animal world already makes sense from God's perspective insofar as it gives him glory and praise.

Praise the Lord from the earth,
you sea monsters and all the deeps of the sea;
Lightning and hail, snow and thick clouds,
storm wind that fulfills his command;
Mountains and all hills, / fruit trees and all cedars;
Animals wild and tame, / creatures that crawl and birds that fly;
Kings of the earth and all peoples,
princes and all who govern on earth;
Young men and women too, / old and young alike.
Let them all praise the Lord's name, / for his name alone is exalted,
His majesty above earth and heaven.
(Psalm 148:7–13)

Creatures praise God in the present age, and they will continue to do so, if God allows, in the age to come. God already delights in the praise of octopuses and chipmunks, and perhaps that is all it takes to make sense of their continued life in heaven, in whatever form God decides that they will take.

NOTES

1. Caroline Walker Bynum, *The Resurrection of the Body in Western Christianity, 200–1336* (New York: Columbia University Press, 1995), 188–90.
2. There are a number of weighty theological issues at stake in this distinction that are beyond the scope of our discussion (for example, and most importantly, the gratuity of grace). For a great overview of the nature/grace distinction, see Stephen Duffy, *The Graced Horizon: Nature and Grace in Modern Catholic Thought* (Collegeville, MN: Liturgical Press, 1992), 50–65.
3. Augustine, "On Grace and Free Will," in *Nicene and Post-Nicene Fathers*, vol. 5, *St. Augustine: Writings Against Pelagius*, ed. Philip Schaff, reprint (Edinburgh: T&T Clark, 1991, [original 1887]), chapter 15, 450.
4. For a discussion of some of the issues at stake here, see Anthony Godzieba, "Bodies and Persons, Resurrected and Postmodern: Toward a Relational Eschatology," in *Theology and Conversation: Towards a Relational Theology*, ed. Jacques Haers and Peter de Mey (Leuven: Peeters, 2003), 211–25.
5. Nathan O'Halloran, "'Each Creature, Resplendently Transfigured': Development of Teaching in *Laudato Si'*," *Theological Studies* 79, no. 2 (June 2018): 376–98.
6. David Vincent Meconi, "Establishing I/Thou Relationship between Creator and Creature," in *On Earth as It Is in Heaven: Cultivating a Contemporary Theology of Creation*, ed. David Vincent Meconi (Grand Rapids: Eerdmans, 2016), 219–36.
7. Ashley Ward, *The Social Lives of Animals* (New York: Basic Books, 2022), 129.

8. Ward, *The Social Lives of Animals*, 232.
9. "Russian Goat Who Made Unlikely Friends with Tiger Dies," Phys.org, November 8, 2019, https://phys.org/news/2019-11-russian-goat-friends-tiger-dies.html.
10. James Dickey, *The Selected Poems* (Middletown, CT: Wesleyan University Press, 1998), 31–32.
11. Eugene Linden, *The Parrot's Lament: And Other True Tales of Animal Intrigue, Intelligence, and Ingenuity* (New York: Penguin Publishing, 2001), 34.
12. *The Parrot's Lament*, 34.
13. Cari Romm, "Can a Predator Really Be Friends with Its Prey? The Murky Science of Interspecies Bonds," *The Atlantic*, December 11, 2015.

FURTHER READING

Many of the sources for this chapter's discussions can be found in *All God's Animals: A Catholic Theological Framework for Animal Ethics*. Washington, DC: Georgetown University Press, 2019, 96–99, 150–155.

Church Documents

The most significant Catholic Church documents are available on the Vatican website, www.vatican.va.

Documents from the Second Vatican Council can be found here: https://www.vatican.va/archive/hist_councils/ii_vatican_council/index.htm.

The Vatican's website has a portal for each pope where their writings, homilies, audiences, and public statements can be found: https://www.vatican.va/holy_father/index.htm.

The *Catechism of the Catholic Church* can be found here: https://www.vatican.va/archive/eng0015/_index.htm.

Nature and Grace

Duffy, Stephen. *The Graced Horizon: Nature and Grace in Modern Catholic Thought*. Collegeville, MN: Liturgical Press, 1992.

Heaven and the Beatific Vision

Boersma, Hans. *Seeing God: The Beatific Vision in Christian Tradition*. Grand Rapids, MI: Eerdmans, 2022.

Papandrea, James L. *What Really Happens after We Die: How We Know There Will Be Hugs in Heaven!* Nashua, NH: Sophia Institute Press, 2019.

Animal Relationships

Dagg, Anne Innis. *Animal Friendships*. New York: Cambridge University Press, 2011.
Haraway, Donna. *When Species Meet*. Minneapolis: University of Minnesota Press, 2007.
Reed, James and Pippa Ehrlich. "My Octopus Teacher." Netflix, September 4, 2020.

PART IV

The Implications for How We Treat Animals

CHAPTER 7

Animal Ethics: Theory

In 2019 Disney released a live-action adaptation of its 1941 movie *Dumbo,* the fantasy story of an elephant with ears big enough to fly. Both versions end with happy elephants. In the 1941 version, Dumbo and his mother stay with the circus. The last scene shows the contented mother riding in the back of a train car with a cheerful Dumbo flying along behind her. In the 2019 version, however, mother and son return to the wild, where they enthusiastically unite with a herd of elephants.

Why the change in endings? I suspect it reflects a societal shift in attitudes about the ethical treatment of animals. Treatments of animals that had been viewed as acceptable (e.g., wild animals in circuses) are now denounced. We find ourselves at a fascinating moment where as a society we are rethinking our answers to some fairly important questions about animals: How should we care for animals? What are the limits of our use of them? And, more broadly, what are our responsibilities to the natural world and why?

In a situation like ours, where cultural norms about an ethical issue are unsettled, ethical theory can help. True, it is not the original wellspring out of which a person's good deeds flow. People do good deeds for a lot of reasons—perhaps they are moved by the plight of others or want to share the blessings they've received with others. But no one's going to say, "I do good deeds because of this great theory I read about." Still, theory has a valuable role. Not only does it help us make sense of our moral intuitions, it also clarifies inconsistencies in our choices so that we can better act in accord with the moral principles we've set for ourselves.

This chapter lays out, on a theoretical level, the ethical implications of the belief that God includes all creation, all animals, in God's salvific plans. In keeping with the Catholic commitment to the reasonableness of moral norms, I suggest that a belief in God's salvific concerns for animals doesn't establish radically new norms but often supports those that are already widely accepted—in society at large but particularly within more animal-friendly quarters. Nonetheless belief in God's salvific embrace of animals does introduce new motivations for acting on those principles along with a readiness to accept more demanding versions of them.

Before making that case, I'll look briefly at a couple of philosophical approaches to animal ethics, followed by an overview of some of the basics of a Catholic approach. Examining these will help us understand how ethical theory works and then, by contrast, identify the distinctive concerns that a belief in God's intent to save *all* creation might bring to our treatment of animals.

PHILOSOPHICAL APPROACHES TO ANIMAL ETHICS

First, a word about ethical theories. In most of our casual conversations with colleagues and friends about what is right or wrong, we make commonsense arguments without explicitly relying on any theoretical framework. We can do this because our culture has some consensus about what forms of behavior are good or evil. Our colleagues generally accept that actions like assisting families in financial straits, giving youth a good education, defending the innocent from those wishing them harm, forgiving a contrite friend, and giving up a bus seat for someone struggling to stand are good things to do. We don't need a theory to show us that. Similarly, we all recognize a number of actions as wrong—making a racist comment, falsely taking credit for another's work, lying to one's spouse, driving dangerously on the road, and violently attacking another for personal gain—without depending on an ethical theory. The devil is in the details, of course, so the more we get into the specifics, the more likely we are to disagree. But a number of moral standards exist that are widely accepted by people of diverse religious and secular worldviews.

At this time, however, cultural views about the right way of treating animals are unsettled. And sometimes inconsistent. Society's moral outrage at cock-fighting rings, for example, is at odds with its resigned tolerance for the plight of factory-farmed chickens, especially given the "inconvenient fact," as anthrozoologist Hal Herzog puts it, "that the life of a fighting cock is fifteen times longer and infinitely more pleasurable than the life of a broiler chicken."[1]

In the midst of this shifting and confused landscape, ethical *theory*, both in its philosophical and religious forms, can make a contribution. Ethical theories don't generate answers that we'll all agree on, but they provide clarity about how and why we arrive at moral judgments. Ethical theories explain our moral beliefs to ourselves and sometimes even challenge those beliefs as wrong. Ethical theories not only help us in deciding which actions are good and which are bad; they also help us understand the basis on which we, typically intuitively, make such judgements.

Constructing an ethical theory involves a bit of circularity. Ethicists develop theories by tacking back and forth between already existing moral views and a theoretical explanation of them. That is, they begin with consensus judgements about the morality of various actions. Then they develop a theory and set of principles that make sense of those judgments, explaining the basis of our moral judgments and what is *really* happening when we decide that something is good. The theories are then tested by looking at sample cases to see if the theories generate expected results. For example, if a proposed ethical theory were to conclude that it is okay to randomly torture innocent people, we would know that the theory doesn't work. However, once we have a theory that's proven itself by its ability to make sense of our common moral beliefs, we can then use it to guide our judgments about other matters—actions whose moral character is not yet clear to us.

Among the ethical theories advanced by philosophers, two of the more common ones are utilitarianism and deontology. (Two other examples are virtue ethics and natural law theory; we'll look at those below.)

Utilitarians hold that the good act is the one that leads to the overall greatest net good. So when faced with a choice about a course of action, we try to figure out what the consequences of each possible course of action will be and then choose the one that leads to better results than all the others.

On first glance, this seems to fit with our basic intuitions; we regularly weigh possible outcomes and balance out competing claims so as to achieve the best results possible in situations where we can't do everything. However, critics argue that the theory leads to conclusions at odds with commonsense moral judgements and therefore is wrong. Utilitarianism seems to demand, for example, that a sheriff *should* falsely accuse an innocent person of a horrible crime if doing so would prevent worse consequences (e.g., a city erupting in violent conflicts because of the crime). The choice confronting the sheriff is either having one innocent individual serve jail time or letting scores of people get injured. The right answer from a utilitarian standpoint, it would seem, is that we falsely accuse the innocent person since doing so leads to better consequences. This we believe to be wrong, and so the theory that generated that conclusion, critics argue, must also be wrong. (Utilitarians believe they have an answer to this, but engaging that debate would lead us too far into the weeds.)

Deontologists (*deon* is Greek for duty) hold that there are some fundamental and universal rules that we are always required to follow; it is our duty, as free and rational beings, to obey these rules. This also seems to align with our intuitions: Certain actions are always wrong regardless of the consequences. We don't torture innocent people just because it will lead to a positive result. But this theory also has its detractors. Traditionally, deontological theories would say that we can never lie (i.e., truth-telling is one of those rules we must always obey). But what if we're hiding a woman from an abusive husband or a child from an angry parent high on drugs? If those intending harm were to ask us whether we are hiding the potential victim of their violence, can we lie? It would seem not. (Deontologists also believe they have an answer to this, but, again, examining those discussions would require more detail than possible here.)

These theories try to explain and systematize already existing judgments about the morality of particular actions—our everyday, commonsense view of what is right and wrong. Again, we typically do not rely on a theory to make moral choices. Most of us reason through our moral decisions without reference to any specific theory; we are instinctively guided by values and goods that most everyone accepts as valid concerns and try to act in accord with them: fairness, kindness, benevolence, justice, and so forth. What ethical theories do is to take these everyday choices and try to make systematic sense of them by explaining what principles undergird them.

Versions of the above two theories have been developed for animal ethics. *Sentient utilitarianism*, in line with the work of the philosopher Peter Singer, maintains that all beings that are sentient and thus able to feel pleasure and pain should be included in utilitarian calculations about what is good and evil.[2] When deliberating about an act, we must consider the good and bad consequences that it has not only for humans but also for animals insofar as they are sentient. Failure to include animals, these advocates argue, is wrong: We arbitrarily prioritize the well-being of one group over all others. Just as racism is morally wrong because it gives preference to certain races, and sexism is wrong because it gives preferences to one gender, so also "speciesism" is wrong because it gives preference to one species (humans) while ignoring others (those made up of sentient animals).

Animal rights ethics is a form of deontology. It argues, following the work of philosopher Tom Regan, that at least some animals are "subjects-of-a-life" (Regan's term). Animals in this category have significant intellectual capabilities such as consciousness, a cognitive capacity to experience pleasure and pain, memory and a sense of the future, and goals and preferences about how to live their lives. Such animals have rights, it is argued, and on that basis, we are prohibited from doing certain things to them. Like human beings, these animals cannot be used merely as a means to an end for the well-being of others. Prohibited acts (e.g., using them for food, clothing, or experiments) are always wrong regardless of how good the consequences might be.

Neither of these theories (sentient utilitarianism or animal rights ethics) reflects our society's dominant sentiment regarding animals. Most people do not believe that animals have civil rights or that we should give proportional consideration to the pleasure and pain of sentient animals. A criticism of these theories, then, is that they are flawed since they do not generate results that fit with our culture's common moral instincts.

However, advocates for these theories push back against this criticism, arguing that the problem lies not with the theories themselves but with our flawed outlook. Our society's moral beliefs about how to treat animals have been distorted by entrenched biases, and thus those beliefs cannot be used as proof that the theories are defective. Self-serving instincts and cultural prejudices (reflected, for example, in the 1941 *Dumbo* movie) have cultivated bad moral intuitions about how to treat animals that these theories are now trying to correct.

These two ethical theories about animals, thus, do not see themselves as advocating a new set of moral norms but rather are exhorting us to apply the *same* moral norms that we are already following, only now without the arbitrary exclusion of nonhumans. The issue, they argue, is one of moral consistency: Sound moral reasoning requires that we follow the *same* logic in making moral judgments about the treatment of *animals* that we are tacitly using when making judgements about *human* affairs.

CATHOLIC ETHICS

Neither of these theories is wholly adequate as a foundation for moral judgments about the treatment of animals, at least from a Catholic standpoint. Nonetheless, I am sympathetic to their conviction that society's conventional beliefs about animal treatment are faulty and need retuning. The challenges that the theories raise against our culture's moral instincts—that animals should not be viewed merely as objects of human interests (in line with an animal rights view) and that the suffering of the more sentient animals is a morally critical factor (in line with sentient utilitarianism)—merit consideration even if not full approval.

Can Catholic ethics be developed in a way that helps us better discern our responsibilities toward animals? I believe it can, but before making that case, it would help to understand some of the essentials of Catholic ethics. Much should be said, but space constraints limit me to a rudimentary sketch of the two theoretical strands that have been influential in the Catholic tradition: natural law and virtue ethics. Neither of these strands is exclusively Catholic; both have other religious and nonreligious versions. Though the two strands are sometimes separated in other moral theories, they have come together in the Catholic tradition as organic parts to form one integral, coherent moral system.

Natural Law

At its heart, Catholic natural law theory is based on an assumption about the world: God has created the world and humanity in such a way that humans are, through the use of their reason, able to discover what is good and evil. In creating the world, God imbued it with his wisdom and gave humanity the capacity to discern that wisdom and understand its practical implications. Thus, for Catholicism, morality is fundamentally rational, accessible to all thinking people. It is not a collection of arbitrary dictates imposed from outside of us (whether by God or some ruling authority), nor does it comprise rules that only the religious insider can know. This commitment to the rationality of ethics has led Catholic thought to be relatively optimistic about the prospect that humans can build consensus across ideological lines about the most important moral beliefs required for a flourishing social life.

Through reason, we develop core principles (e.g., protecting human life is good, families and the education of children are good, and social existence is good) and apply these principles to ever new and changing circumstances. With this commitment to the reasonableness of moral norms, the Catholic tradition has generally avoided the view that some activities are wrong simply because God has prohibited them. Actions are wrong because they go against what is reasonable, and our reason tells us as much.

Or at least it does when it is working well. As a consequence of the Fall, our capacity to reason has been wounded, and our sinful biases and desires interfere with moral judgments. Nonetheless, our capacity to reason has not been destroyed, and thus it is still possible for us to arrive at correct moral judgments, at least in our better moments. Catholicism believes that revelation and church teaching assist us by providing general moral norms that reflect the best of human wisdom and help keep our moral reasoning on the right path. At the same time, the Catholic tradition has long recognized that the more we get into the details, the more likely it is that we'll err, and the Church generally avoids judgments about such details. For example, we can all affirm a general moral principle that it is wrong for one small group to possess the vast majority of a nation's riches without agreeing on what is the best strategy for redressing that injustice when it occurs.

Virtue Ethics

Catholic virtue ethics developed out of Aquinas's engagement with the Greek philosopher Aristotle. Virtue ethics centers on what it considers the end point of human life, its ideal form, and maintains that actions are good insofar as they help us grow as persons toward that end point. The ideal form of human life entails living in a way that accords with reason, within a harmonious and just society, bonded together in relationships with similarly virtuous neighbors, and ultimately, for the Christian, united in loving communion with God. Few of us lead such a life, but correct choices about how to act move us closer to it.

Good actions bring us closer to our end because they shape us—shape each person's character and the emotions and dispositions that underlie that character. All of our actions, whether good or bad, leave traces on our character. They foster in us certain habits, inclinations toward acting in a certain way. When we repeatedly do an act that is good (virtuous)—for example, being patient with the foibles of others—we become more disposed toward that good act. It becomes easier for us to be patient, and thus we become virtuous in a particular way (i.e., we become patient persons). Similarly, when we repeatedly act in a bad way—for example, telling self-serving lies—we form in ourselves a vice. We become liars. Our actions shape us into good (virtuous) or bad (vicious) people. This is true for all virtuous dispositions. Acting in ways that are just, to offer another example, helps us become attuned, rationally and affectively, to the requirements of justice, and thus our passions are less likely to lead our reasoning astray. Conversely, acts of injustice deform our moral instincts and further amplify sinful inclinations to oppress others and be unjust. The goal of the moral life, therefore, is not just to do good acts but to become truly good, virtuous people.

Animals and Catholic Ethics

A word at this point about how Catholicism has traditionally understood our ethical duty toward animals. That duty is informed by both of the two traditions above, the rationality of natural law and the virtuous dispositions of virtue ethics. However, following Aquinas, most Catholic thinkers have traditionally maintained that we do not have a *direct* moral duty toward animals. Rather we have a duty to *ourselves* to be rational and act virtuously. Since acting cruelly to animals is not rational, persons doing such an act would be violating their dignity as a rational being. We saw this view in the *Catechism*: "It is *contrary to human dignity* to cause animals to suffer or die needlessly" (no. 2418, emphasis added).

Now the idea that we do not have a direct duty to animals seems at odds with common sense. Cruelty to an animal is first and foremost a harm to the animal itself, not human dignity. However, Aquinas, who was influential in shaping Catholic thought on this point, maintained that we cannot genuinely love animals for their own sake or have them as a direct object of our moral concern. We can only love animals indirectly, insofar as "we regard them as the good things that we desire for others" (Aquinas, *Summa Theologiae*, II-II.25.3) So, I can love my friend's dog but only because of the happiness it brings her, not for its own sake.

Interestingly, one of the arguments Aquinas uses to defend his view here depends on his belief that animals won't be in heaven with us. "Charity," love directed toward the other, "is based on the fellowship of everlasting happiness, to which the irrational creature cannot attain" (Aquinas, *Summa Theologiae*, II-II.25.3). That is, since animals (irrational creatures) will not join us in the fellowship of heaven, we cannot have a loving relationship with them in the here and now. Given this book's hope that animals *will* join us in the life to come, we can follow his argument to a different conclusion: Because animals will share with us in the fellowship of heaven, we *can* love them in the present age.

THE KINGDOM OF GOD

The integration of these two ethical theories—natural law and virtue ethics—has shaped Catholic ethical theory at least since the Middle Ages. Recently, however, a new wrinkle has been introduced. In the first half of the twentieth century, a number of Catholic ethicists criticized the prevailing approaches in Catholic ethics as being too rationalistic and not sufficiently informed by the Gospel of Jesus Christ. In short, Catholic morality wasn't, they argued, Christian enough.

In response Vatican II called for Catholic morality to be "nourished more on the teaching of the Bible" so that it will "shed light on the loftiness of the calling of the faithful in Christ" (*Optatam Totius*, §16). Christians are to be like Christ and live out his lofty ideals of love and not be limited to conventional ideas about what is good or loving. One way that scholars and church leaders have addressed this call for a more biblical and Christian-specific ethics has been to situate Catholic ethics in the context of the kingdom of God.

The inauguration of the kingdom of God was central to Jesus's preaching. If one includes cognates of the term (e.g., "kingdom of heaven" and "reign of God"), references to the kingdom of God occur more than one hundred times in the Gospels,[3] and, of course, the plea for its coming is prominent in the central Christian prayer: "Our Father, who art in heaven, hallowed be thy name; thy kingdom come; thy will be done on earth as it is in heaven." Jesus begins his ministry with the proclamation that "the time of fulfillment" has come and that "the kingdom of God is at hand" (Mark 1:15). The kingdom is precious, something that awakens our desires and hopes: "The kingdom of heaven is like a treasure buried in a field" (Matthew 13:45). The kingdom of God has already been inaugurated in Jesus's ministry: "The kingdom of God has come upon you" (Luke 17:20–21). And yet its fullness is not yet here. Jesus describes the kingdom as a mustard seed, tiny among seeds but one that will grow into the largest of shrubs. And in John's Gospel, Jesus tells Pilate that "my kingdom does not belong to this world" (John 18:36).

Thus the Gospels portray the kingdom of God as a reality that is both already present in Jesus's ministry *and* yet something still to come. Scholars use the phrase "already and not yet" to describe this dual aspect of the kingdom. Through word and deed, Christ inaugurated the kingdom of God (it has "already" begun), but its fullness will only appear at the end times when Christ returns and completes God's plan (and thus it is "not yet"). Until the Second Coming of Jesus, Christians live between the times—between the "already" of the kingdom that has been inaugurated in Christ and the "not yet" of the kingdom whose fullness will appear only when Jesus returns.[4] The already/not yet tension is peculiar to the Christian worldview and to how Christians are to act in the world. Christian ethics looks to the witness of Christ's life and his teachings and assesses how they can be embodied within a particular historical context.

Though often expressed in demanding forms, the values that animated Jesus's life are truly *human* values and, in that sense, are reasonable and often common to all people of good will. Those values can be found throughout

Jesus's life and preaching, but Christians have long given chapters 5 through 7 of Matthew's Gospel a privileged status. The section begins with the well-known beatitudes ("blessed are the poor in spirit, . . . blessed are they who mourn, . . . blessed are the meek . . ."). The section continues with what some scholars term the "hard sayings"—a collection of statements that are among the most challenging made by Jesus about the demands of genuine love and true holiness.

> And if your right hand causes you to sin, cut it off and throw it away . . . offer no resistance to one who is evil. . . . When someone strikes you on [your] right cheek, turn the other one to him as well. . . . If anyone wants to go to law with you over your tunic, hand him your cloak as well. . . . love your enemies, and pray for those who persecute you. . . . So, be perfect, just as your heavenly Father is perfect. . . . Do not store up for yourselves treasures on earth. . . . But store up treasures in heaven. . . . do not worry about your life, what you will eat [or drink], or about your body, what you will wear. . . . Stop judging, that you may not be judged. . . . Do to others whatever you would have them do to you. (Matthew 5:30–7:12)

And yet, even while aspiring to the ideals indicated by these hard sayings, the Christian also recognizes that social conditions and human limits will mean that those ideals cannot be, and even should not be, always pursued. Valiant soldiers sometimes need to use violence to defend the innocent. Indiscriminate sharing of one's goods will likely lead to one's own impoverishment. Forgiveness and mercy in business matters are appropriate at times but would cause financial ruin as a regular practice.

So, on the one hand, the kingdom of God—one of peace, reconciliation, harmony, sharing, mutuality, justice, and love—has started in Christ's life, and therefore the Christian should be fervent in making the kingdom present through acts of forgiveness and mercy, service to the needy, and the labor for justice. And yet, on the other hand, the kingdom is not here in its fullness, and thus sometimes acts like violence, a refusal to share, and protection of one's own professional interests are necessary.[5]

If it is the case, as this book argues, that animals are to be included in the age to come and therefore share in the fellowship of the kingdom—"the fellowship of everlasting happiness," to use Aquinas's phrase—then our attempts to live lives that anticipate the peaceable harmony of the kingdom should include them. To exclude animals from our concerns for the kingdom would effectively sunder it, cordoning off its nonhuman realm from its human one, both in regard to how those realms are foreshadowed in the present age and how we understand their fulfillment in the age to come. That view, however, clashes with both the biblical narrative and recent papal teaching; neither of them provides a basis for fragmenting the created order or God's plans for it. God's salvific plan is directed toward all creation; its goal is to integrate all things, human and nonhuman, into Christ. Certainly distinctions can be made—*must* be made—between human and nonhuman creatures along with God's respective plans for each and our duties in serving those plans. But those distinctions nonetheless are directed toward an integral and unified whole, one whose summit and meaning lies in Christ and the Gospel values he proclaimed.

To accept creation and the animals within it as fellow participants in the kingdom requires a shift in attitude. It is not just that we should act differently, better, toward animals. We should also move away from an attitude that sees animals as "out there," removed from us. Instead the Christian is called to view them through the lens of the kingdom, as creatures already integrally related to us and in communion with us. That our practices toward animals like pigs, mice, and cows rarely conform to the ideals of the kingdom could be the result of valid human need for which animals are still required. But it also seems possible that another factor is at play: an enduring legacy of historical attitudes that has insulated our treatment of animals from the discomforting standard of the kingdom.

ANIMALS AND THE ALREADY/NOT YET OF THE KINGDOM

The Christian commitment to the kingdom leads us to a corrective swerve in what it means to act as good people, pushing our moral lives beyond a cultural standard of goodness and toward the one set by Christ. This moral stretching applies first and foremost to how we treat other humans but also, *mutatis mutandis*, to how we treat animals. At the same time, the already/not yet of the kingdom also helps us understand why attempts to live in accord with the kingdom will be frustrated. Until the fullness of the kingdom arrives, the world's brokenness will thwart its ideals.

For now, conflicts with nonhuman creatures ("enmity," to use the language of Genesis 3:15) are unavoidable. Against what might be understood as the ideals of the kingdom, we allow ourselves, rightly, to prevent the flourishing of some creatures. Webworms living in our pecan trees, foxes seeking prey in human habitats, pigeons hovering at the town square eateries, mice desiring the warmth of our homes, and ticks using us as food banks: We believe ourselves justified in refusing to share our goods with nonhuman creatures.

We have an ethical duty to try and act in accord with the kingdom in our interactions with animals, but that's not always possible or wise. The perplexities involved are more than can be detailed here, but a few general observations about two categories of animal ecosystems, domesticated animals and wildlife, can give us a sense of the issues confronting us.

The domestication of animals—cows, sheep, pigs, horses, chickens, goats, dogs, cats, and so forth—has allowed us to form relationships with at least some animals that can be good and life-giving, for both the animals and us. The values of the kingdom can be applied more easily to our treatment of them than is the case for animals in the wild. Their proximity to us, the history of human experience about how to intervene helpfully in their lives, and the managerial control we often have over their circumstances mean that we are able to care for them with insight and wisdom—acting in ways that alleviate their fear, anxiety, and hunger and that encourage the particular form of sociality and flourishing that is appropriate for their species. Our response to these animals might be described as eschatological in that by tending to these animals with kindness and compassion, we anticipate the kingdom whose fullness we await. Nurturing care for domestic animals fosters the harmony we expect to be part of the kingdom's life, and thus we can and should view such care as part of the Christian's participation in the labor for the kingdom.

Nonetheless we cannot romanticize even this subset of animal relationships. In the limited ecosystems of domesticated animals, Christians will still face difficult situations because of the "not yet" of the kingdom. The interests and needs of the animals will sometimes conflict with those of humans, forcing a hard choice between two goods that cannot both be realized. That conflict is fundamental to all uses of domestic animals for food, labor, and experiments.

A different set of issues confront us in the case of animals in the wilderness. Based on the ideals of a harmonious kingdom, a few brave souls have argued that we should seek out ways to transform, someday, wildlife ecosystems so that they are more reflective of the kingdom. Since God does not desire the suffering of animals, we should work, the argument goes, toward a future where the reduction of predation and other forms of animal violence becomes a possibility. While I laud the goal, it is unrealistic. Eliminating suffering in the wild is not feasible in the present or proximate future and would probably be unwise to attempt even if opportunities arose. The vastness of the world's ecosystems and the extent of their internal complexities are such that even the smallest of them is beyond our capacity to understand or control. And in our ignorance and hubris, any intervention to modify them seems likely to cause unintended consequences. For now reducing the natural violence of the wild must wait upon God's intervention.

Nevertheless a response from the Christian community is still possible and required, one that draws on its own theological perspective in ways that will sometimes complement reigning cultural values and at other times be at odds with them. Justifications for protecting the wilderness and the animals in it often center on human need—the aesthetic delight of the natural world, the recreational entertainment it brings, and the possibility that one of its inhabitants might hold a cure for some human ailment. The Church accepts these arguments, but as Pope Francis reminds us, God has other interests in these animals besides that of serving human need: They praise God, and he delights in them. And if the arguments so far have merit, God will, in the kingdom that is come, continue to delight in these animals and the ecosystems that they inhabit. Thus in their present beauty and splendor, they foreshadow the glory of God's kingdom.

As creation's steward, the Christian is responsible for protecting these divine interests. The Christian community does not reject anthropocentric concerns, but its response to animals in the wild is principally elicited by a different kind of inspiration, a deep religious affection for the natural world ultimately rooted in creation's theological import: It is cherished by God. In efforts to establish and maintain parks, preserves, and other forms of protected areas, the Christian is responding to a divine calling; they act in fidelity to the joint tasks of stewarding creation and laboring for the kingdom.

Finally, one subcategory of wildlife merits special attention: animals that have a hostile relationship with humans because of their proximity to us. These creatures are in various degrees dangerous (snakes), unhealthy (mice), nuisances (opossums), or some combination of the above. Given the distinctive value of human persons, it is appropriate that we protect ourselves from animal threats, even when doing so entails violence. Nonetheless the options for resolving human–animal conflicts are often multiple, with tradeoffs for the humans and animals involved, and these warrant discernment. What is convenient and cheap for a frustrated human might be cruel to an animal (e.g., glue traps for mice). In such situations, we might push ourselves to pursue more costly or inconvenient strategies if doing so allows us to better embody the values of the kingdom.

In sum, our actions toward animals will sometimes, necessarily, reflect the "not yet" of the kingdom and a falling away from the ideals it represents. It is not possible in this world, because of human finitude and the conflicts between goods characteristic of a broken world, to actualize in any given act or set of practices all the values that we associate with the kingdom, and thus we will be forced to act in ways that are at odds with them. An example of these limits appears in the long history of human need for animals to survive, a need that sometimes required—especially before the domestication of animals—hunting animals with primitive instruments that inflicted significant torment on them. Our approval of such historical practices reflects the valid belief that there are circumstances—increasingly rare, one hopes—where human well-being justifies the painful and deadly treatment of animals.

Nonetheless, in the contained and manageable ecosystems comprising human and domesticated animals, Christians will have opportunities to witness to the kingdom: to rethink what it means to have dominion over animals and create a space for animals to flourish. This will require a change in attitude, moving from an emphasis on control and productivity to one more attuned to the compassionate governance of God, seeing in the comparative weakness, vulnerability, and voicelessness of domestic animals a symbol of God's poor and embracing them as members of our community, whenever and however appropriate and possible.

THE VOCATION OF THE CHRISTIAN: A UNIVERSAL AND PERSONAL CALLING

All Christians individually and the Church as a whole should witness to the kingdom in its care for animals. "With the help of God's grace, [the Christian] cooperates in the growth of the kingdom, until the historical and eschatological fulfillment" of God's plan (John Paul II, "Audience," June 18, 1986). This cooperation with God's plan includes both practical actions on behalf of animals and, as we saw in chapter 5, our prayers for them.

Because of the task that God has bestowed on the Church, that of laboring for the kingdom, the Christian community is to care for creation in a manner that helps lead it to the destiny intended by God. We see this in the writings of popes John Paul II, Benedict XVI, and Francis; Christians are called to be stewards of God's plan for creation. Recognizing that God has given humanity a distinctive role should *increase* our concern for creatures that are vulnerable and have no other advocate. Because of the particular gifts that God has bestowed upon humanity, we have the privilege of doing what no other creature is able to do: exercise the kind of self-giving leadership displayed in Jesus's life.

Christian care for creation is part of the universal calling to follow Christ that is shared by all Christians, and thus is part of the common set of moral norms that govern all Christians. Nonetheless each Christian will embody these common Christian norms in different ways.[6] This is partly because each of us is limited (no one of us can do everything). But in addition, God's calling is also personal, addressed to the individual person and calling forth the distinctive goodness that God created that person to be. Because no one individual's life can fully express the kingdom, the Christian vocation will take myriad forms, as the lives of the 10,000-plus Catholic saints well attest: contemplative devotion (St. Thérèse of Lisieux), worker solidarity (Servant of God Dorothy Day), martyrdom in the cause of justice (St. Óscar Romero), the rejection of violence (St. Martin of Tours), and, of course, evangelical care for nonhuman creatures (St. Francis of Assisi).

Similarly, though an individual Christian's responsibilities toward animals will always include both praying for creation (an ever-present task for the Christian) and acting in ways that conform to universal norms (e.g., animal abuse is always to be rejected and compassionate care encouraged), their personal witnesses to the kingdom might lead them to respond creatively based on their distinctive gifts and how God calls them.[7] Given the enormity of human suffering and the demands we face in responding to it, it is understandable that for many Christians their care for creation and the animals within it might consist simply in cultivating modest practices that avoid further harm to the natural world and the animals in it. But because God will stir up energies and passions for Christians to labor for the kingdom in different ways, Christian care for animals will appear in a complex variety of both mundane and dramatic forms as individuals respond to God's distinctive call to each of them and in doing so advance the Church's universal, salvific mission.

Christian discipleship will often require more than just following universal norms, and correspondingly God may call a person—require of them—actions that God does not require of others. All Christians are bound by universal norms and the basic responsibilities of the Christian life, but it is likely that an individual will have duties that go beyond these because of God's personal call to that individual. This is something that St. Ignatius of Loyola well understood. God's call is addressed to the individual at a concrete time and in a particular situation. Therefore, a Christian's choice will sometimes require discernment about what God's distinctive will is for them in that particular moment in history.[8] The Christian will be drawn by the Spirit to surrender their particular talents, distinctive agency, and moral energies to God in Christlike discipleship. Every Christian is required to do *something*, but not the *same* something. We are all required to work for the kingdom, but not in the same way.

CONCLUSION

Most of us do not need an ethical theory to help us decide what is right or wrong. But theory is important in that it clarifies the principles that are already shaping some of our moral intuitions and the ways that those same intuitions might be wrong. Catholicism, with its embrace of the natural law tradition, has long affirmed the fundamental rationality of moral actions, which it has understood in the context of our virtuous end (i.e., a rationally ordered social life before God).

The kingdom of God does not overturn the values at stake in this moral framework, but it can and often does radicalize them. Acts of self-giving generosity—financial support for the poor, emotional support for those grieving, costly fidelity to moral principles—are core tasks in the Christian's becoming a Christlike witness to the kingdom. Yet we are limited creatures living in a broken world that awaits the final transformation of the kingdom, and so our actions will sometimes fall short of its ideals.

If animals are to be part of that future kingdom, then building the kingdom on earth requires that we include them in our prayerful imaginings about how God's reign can grow in this particular moment in history. The kingdom's status as already/not yet means that we should feel the attractive pull of Gospel ideals even while recognizing the human and structural limits of the present age. Avoiding both naïve idealism and skeptical cynicism, we strive with hope to embody, in the present age, relationships with animals that reflect the ideals of that kingdom in whatever ways that opportunity and God's grace allow.

NOTES

1. Hal Herzog, *Some We Love, Some We Hate, Some We Eat: Why It's So Hard to Think Straight about Animals* (New York: Harper, 2010), 170.
2. Peter Singer, *Animal Liberation: The Definitive Classic of the Animal Movement*, rev. ed. (New York: Open Road Media, 2015).
3. Richard Middleton, *A New Heaven and a New Earth: Reclaiming Biblical Eschatology* (Grand Rapids: Baker Academic, 2014), 245.
4. See Christoph Schwöbel, "Last Things First: The Century of Eschatology in Retrospect," in *The Future as God's Gift: Explorations in Christian Eschatology*, ed. Marcel Sarot and David Fergusson (Edinburgh: T & T Clark, 2000), 217–41.
5. For more on this tension as it relates to violence, see Lisa Sowle Cahill, *Love Your Enemies: Discipleship, Pacifism, and Just War Theory* (Minneapolis: Fortress Press, 1994), 15–38.
6. Gilbert Meilaender, "Is What Is Right for Me Right for All Persons Similarly Situated?," *The Journal of Religious Ethics* 8, no. 1 (1980): 125–34.

7. The "Christian life is not merely satisfying universal norms." Karl Rahner, *Foundations of Christian Faith: An Introduction to the Idea of Christianity*, trans. William V. Dych (New York: Crossroad, 1996), 311.
8. Mark Thibodeaux, SJ, *Armchair Mystic: How Contemplative Prayer Can Lead You Closer to God* (Cincinnati, OH: Franciscan Media, 2019).

FURTHER READING

Many of the sources for this chapter's discussions can be found in chapter 5 of *All God's Animals: A Catholic Theological Framework for Animal Ethics*. Washington, DC: Georgetown University Press, 2019, 171–212.

Catholic Ethics

Keenan, James F. *A History of Catholic Theological Ethics*. Mahwah, NJ: Paulist, 2022.

Massaro, Thomas. *Living Justice: Catholic Social Teaching in Action*, third ed. Lanham, MD: Rowan & Littlefield Publishers, 2015.

Kingdom Ethics

Gushee, David P. and Glen H. Stassen. *Kingdom Ethics: Following Jesus in Contemporary Context*. Grand Rapids, MI: Eerdmans, 2017.

Animal Ethics: Christian Approaches

Clough, David. *On Animals*. Vol. 2. *Theological Ethics*. New York: T&T Clark, 2018.

York, Tripp and Andy Alexis-Baker, eds. *A Faith Embracing All Creatures: Addressing Commonly Asked Questions about Christian Care for Animals*. Eugene, OR: Cascade Books, 2012.

Linzey, Andrew and Dorothy Yamamoto, eds. *Animals on the Agenda: Questions about Animals for Theology and Ethics*. Urbana, IL: University of Illinois Press, 1998.

Pinches, Charles and Jay B. McDaniel, eds. *Good News for Animals? Christian Approaches to Animal Well-Being*. New York: Orbis Books, 1993.

Animal Ethics: Interreligious and Interdisciplinary Approaches

Sideris, Lisa H. *Environmental Ethics, Ecological Theology, and Natural Selection*. New York: Columbia University Press, 2003.

Waldau, Paul and Kimberley C. Patton, eds. *A Communion of Subjects: Animals in Religion, Science, and Ethics*. New York: Columbia University Press, 2006.

Animal Ethics: Philosophical Approaches

Regan, Tom. *The Case for Animal Rights*. Berkeley: University of California Press, 1983.
Singer, Peter. *Animal Liberation*, rev. ed. New York: Open Road Media, 2015.

CHAPTER 8

Animal Ethics: Applied

For a brief, 24-hour news cycle in 2014, the world believed that Pope Francis had declared that pets will go to heaven. The news spread quickly through a surge of clickbait headlines, some in major media: *The New York Times* ("Dogs in Heaven? Pope Francis Leaves Pearly Gates Open"); *USA Today* ("Pope Francis Says That Dogs Can Go to Heaven"); *Time Magazine* ("Pope Francis Says There's a Place for Pets in Paradise"); and CNN ("Pope Francis Says That Dogs Can Go to Heaven"). To the dismay of the dog-loving globe, the media got it wrong (likely due to a mistranslation of an Italian story). Though the claim was unfounded, the spirited reaction to it shows just how much people mourn the loss of companion animals and yearn to see them again in the next life. Understandably so.

Overlooked, however, in this frenzied concern for the eternal destiny of one group of animals was the eternal plight of all the others that are part of our lives—those that provide us food, enable new medical insights, give us pleasure in hunting them, or annoy us to the point of setting traps for them. Perhaps God approves of our decidedly preferential care for some animals over others. Still, it seems likely that the measure of an authentically Christ-like care for animals lies not in how well we love our companion animals but in whether and how we attend to those animals at the margins of our culture's concern, those whose suffering is less visible and more easily ignored—the delicious pigs in our factory farms and the servile mice in our laboratories.

This final chapter establishes some basic principles that follow upon the belief that all creation is included in God's salvific plans. Because nonhuman creatures are genuine objects of God's salvific care, we can hope that they, or at least many of them, will join us in the kingdom of God. Our response to them, therefore, should be instructed by Christianity's vision of that future life and its values (i.e., a life centered on loving, harmonious relationships). Given God's covenantal interest, our care will privilege the animals that are most capable of forming genuine relationships with people and with other animal creatures (cats, baboons, seals, and crows). Such animals have what can be described as more "covenantal potential," more of a capacity to relate to others than less developed creatures (starfish and earthworms). This covenantal potential justifies differences in how we respond to animal needs. Because animals have varied capacities for relationships with others, our ethical responses to them will, appropriately, vary depending on whether we are dealing with butterflies or baboons, blue jays or beetles.

PRINCIPLES FOR ANIMALS ETHICS

Based on discussions in the previous chapters, I offer the following ten principles to frame a Catholic approach to animal ethics. I group them into two categories: (1) a Catholic theology of animals, and (2) the ethical response generated by that theology.

A Catholic Theology of Animals

The basis for the theological vision presented here is the belief that God labors to draw all creation to fulfillment and that he calls all of us to join him in that labor. Two complementary themes guide my understanding of God's goal in this labor: the covenant and the kingdom of God. The covenant underscores the central importance of relationality in God's hope for all creation, and the kingdom highlights the ideal of a just, interconnected, and harmonious order of creatures flourishing within God's reign. Humans, animals, plants, rivers, and mountains: We're all in this together because God wants us to be together.

Scripture promises that God will draw *all* things together in the Son. The triune God of the covenant has a salvific tenderness toward each and every creature and includes them in his covenantal plans for creation. My theological understanding of animals is informed by this inclusion and, in turn, by the life of the kingdom inasmuch as animals will be co-sharers in it. Animals are not temporary tools for human use, needed now but to be discarded in the next age. God created them for their distinctive goodness and beauty and intends that they join him in heaven. Animals will be with us as part of an interconnected ecosystem in heaven, one healed of all wounds, with all creatures participating in a community of eternal fellowship and play, forever bonded to Christ, their lord and companion, and turned to the Father who created them in endless praise.

Humanity has a special role in bringing about God's plan for creation. In granting us dominion over the creatures of the world, God intended that we would be his representatives on earth, acting as stewards of creation and agents of the budding of the kingdom.

With these reflections in mind, I offer five principles for a Catholic theology of animals.

1. The ultimate purpose and value of animals is not that of serving human need.
2. Because of humanity's privileged status as bearers of the *imago Dei* and stewards of creation, God has granted it a limited dominion over animals.
3. Each animal is lovingly created by God in order for it to live within a web of relationships—with us, with other creatures, and ultimately with God.
4. God's goal in Christ is to heal and ultimately restore and elevate these interconnected bonds and the animals within them.
5. The values of the kingdom (justice, mercy, care) and the capabilities that give rise to rich covenantal relationships (subjectivity, capacity for friendship, self-awareness) are important goods in God's plan for creation.

The Christian Ethical Response

The two themes, the kingdom and the covenant, give rise to two sets of goods and values that Christians should consider in all their moral choices. The kingdom has begun in Christ, and thus Christians are to see the world in terms of the possibilities for that kingdom in the present age. God has tasked the Church with continuing Christ's work by making his kingdom real in the midst of a broken world. Since animals are to be part of that kingdom, this work includes care for them. When we care for animals, we are doing God's work.

The covenant underscores the importance of relationality for God. As Christians view animals in light of the kingdom, they will give serious consideration to the value of all relationships and to those goods that make deep and rich relationships possible—for example, sentience, a sense of self that endures across time, compassion for another, the capacity for mutuality, and so forth.

This means that we should resist a human/nonhuman binary insofar as it places all nonhumans in the same ethical category and should instead give the more cognitively developed animals privileged concern in our ethical deliberations. Humans retain their unique status, but our responses to other animals should be shaped by the distinctive capacities, needs, and desires of the animal under consideration.

Complementing this newly complicated discernment directed toward the *individual* animal, concern for advancing the kingdom also draws Christian focus on the good of creation's *communal*, ecological whole and encourages Christians, as creation's stewards, to promote the ecological goods necessary for a flourishing and harmonious communal life among all creatures, human and nonhuman. Given the lived location of most animals, our service to the kingdom will entail responsibility for preserving the ecosystems in which they presently participate.

However, because the kingdom has not yet arrived in its fullness, important goods will come into conflict, leading to situations where Christians must sacrifice some goods (e.g., those related to animal well-being) in order to achieve others (human flourishing). While such acts (e.g., setting mouse traps, eating animal flesh, conducting animal experiments) are sometimes justified, they are not activities that God originally intended when giving humanity dominion over other creatures. Nor do they reflect God's ultimate hope for nonhuman creatures.

Since what is at stake is an earthly and religious reality, Christian labors for animals have both practical and prayerful dimensions. Christians are to serve the kingdom through their actions, and they are also to lift up in prayerful petition their hope for God's saving intervention.

Generating specific norms for the concrete care of animals beyond general principles is difficult. The needs are many and pressing, and thus the opportunities for serving the kingdom are virtually limitless. Though Christians will sometimes allow more practical considerations to inform their labors, ultimately their service will keep stretching toward the ideals of the kingdom in accord with grace and God's personal call to each of them.

On the basis of these reflections, I'll suggest five principles for understanding the Christian ethical response to animals.

1. The Church is to be the agent of the kingdom, reflecting the servant model of Christ's ministry as it continues his salvific work. In this labor, the Christian is to act, whenever and however possible, in ways that accord with an animal's species-specific form of flourishing and that reflect the standards of the kingdom. Because the well-being of

many animals depends on the health of their ecosystems, those systems become an appropriate focus of Christian care and concern.
2. As with all its labors, the Church's care for animals should be expressed not only in the practical care that it shows animals but also in its prayer for them.
3. All Christians are called to labor for creation, but God will call each Christian to do so in distinctive ways.
4. Christian discernment about moral practices should be guided by consideration of the values of the covenant (relationality, communion) and the ideals of the kingdom (harmony, nonviolence). Attending to these values and ideals, however, will make moral clarity difficult given the myriad ways that they impinge on a particular situation or context.
5. Acts that, with moral justification, inflict suffering on animals or compromise their flourishing should be seen as a consequence of humanity's limited dominion over creation and the fact that the kingdom has not come in its fullness.

The practices resulting from the above will not, typically, entail a radical departure from the more animal-friendly social norms that have developed in recent decades. This is to be expected given Catholicism's belief in the fundamental reasonableness of ethics. Indeed, these practices will often align with the basic commitments of many animal advocates of whatever religious or secular stripe and the sentiments of ordinary Christians. Everyday care and kindness toward animals, especially those with developed cognition, are foundational, though they are only a starting point.

Perhaps the most impactful change introduced by the above is that care for animals now becomes part of the unbounded demands of the Gospel as reflected in the beatitudes and the hard sayings. These demands, always and relentlessly, push us forward, urging us to become more generous and Christlike. Self-righteous complacency about our moral goodness should always be rejected.

Prayerful Christians already sense this in regard to their neighbor; there is always more that can be done. But given God's intent to save all creation, any complacent satisfaction we might have about our care for animals and their ecosystems is likewise excluded. Christians must take seriously the responsibility of caring for animals, must see such care not as an occasional duty incumbent on all good people but as a pressing requirement of the Gospel. Care for animals cannot be given the same moral weight as love for the human neighbor, of course, but it is, nonetheless, part of the broader Christian task of laboring for the kingdom. With saints like Philip Neri, the Christian can and should see acts of gentleness, mercy, and kindness toward animals as expressions of Christian discipleship and responses to the call of Jesus. Moreover, some Christians will, no doubt, be called to continue Neri's saintly legacy through a more radical witness to the kingdom's compassion for animals.

Because the above principles approach animal care through the lens of Gospel values, they arouse prayerful scrutiny of any action that inflicts suffering and violence on animals in order to serve human pleasure. Included in this category are, of course, animal sports fights, but we might also consider—when pursued only for pleasure and not genuine need—hunting, fishing, and eating foie gras and veal. Any human enjoyment that directly depends on animal suffering is, at first glance, at odds with the world that God desires and the final liberation that awaits in the full coming of the kingdom. Though Christians should resist engaging in such practices simply for pleasure, I recognize that entertaining activities will sometimes overlap with important human interests (cultural, familial, and civic). Such human interests are appropriate considerations, though they should be used cautiously and not as facile justifications for regular departures from the kingdom's ideals.

Other forms of animal suffering are inflicted not for human enjoyment but for reasons of health and healing. These are vital practices and are often unavoidable at this time in human history (e.g., withdrawing the blood of horseshoe crabs for vaccines, using mice for experiments, the culling of animals to prevent the outbreak of disease). However, even these practices should be recurrently examined to ensure that less violent alternatives are not available. What Pope John Paul II said about animal experimentation—"the diminution of experimentation on animals corresponds to the plan and well-being of all creation" ("Address to Scientists," October 23, 1982)—applies to all actions that inflict suffering on animals in the name of human need. We should continually seek their diminution and, ultimately, their elimination. In line with John Paul's teaching, we can say that any work to diminish animal suffering without undermining vital human needs contributes to the building of the kingdom.

In order to provide examples of the ethical discernment informed by these principles, I examine two cases. The reflections on each will, necessarily, be brief and tentative.

EATING MEAT FROM FACTORY FARMS

The term "factory farming" loosely refers to large-scale operations that are driven by a desire to maximize meat production with little regard for animal welfare. Common estimates are that 95% or more of the meat we eat comes from such operations. Slaughtering animals for food has always been part of human existence, but for most of that history, animals lived fairly good and natural lives until the day of their slaughter. That has changed over the past half century. As factory farming has come to dominate, few of the animals we eat live lives that are natural or free of anguish.[1]

I know of no ethicist who defends factory farming. Simply, the suffering that it inflicts on animals in order to deliver cheap meat is appalling and horrific.

> Cheap meat comes at a cost. A broiler chicken's bones cannot keep up with the explosive growth of its body. Unnaturally large breasts torque a chicken's legs, causing lameness, ruptured tendons, and twisted leg syndrome. . . . Arthritis, heart disease, sudden death syndrome, and a host of metabolic disorders are prevalent among industrial broilers.[2]

The living conditions of factory-farmed chickens are "Dante-esque." They spend most of their days "lying down, often in litter contaminated with excrement. As a result, many will develop breast blisters, hock burns, and sores on their feet." The air they breathe is "laced with ammonia produced by the action of microbes on the accumulated urine and the excrement of tens of thousands of birds," burning the lungs and the eyes.[3] Understandably, Pope Benedict criticized factory farming before his elevation to the papacy: "Certainly, a sort of industrial use of creatures, so that . . . hens live so packed together that they become just caricatures of birds, *this degrading of living creatures to a commodity* seems to me in fact to contradict the relationship of mutuality that comes across in the Bible."[4]

In the last chapter, we saw that for a virtue ethics approach, good actions foster a virtuous character in us, while bad actions do the opposite. Within that ethical framework, serious questions can be raised about factory farming given its morally corrosive effect on workers. One "sticker," the worker responsible for cutting the animal's carotid arteries and a jugular vein in its neck, recounts the heavy toll that the slaughterhouse takes on its workers. He was fortunate; Alcoholics Anonymous had given him an outlet where he "could go to people and talk to them." A lot of his coworkers, however, "just drink and drug their problems away," and "end up abusing their spouses because they can't get rid of the feelings."[5] The psychological toll likely explains the findings of one study; it showed that the presence of slaughterhouses correlates with increased violent crime in the surrounding area.[6]

Most of the meat we eat is produced in similar slaughterhouses, places of misery for animals and workers alike, with baneful consequences that ripple throughout the surrounding community. We can ask, as members of a culture that tacitly supports such systems through its meat purchases, how their existence can be reconciled with the devotion we otherwise feel for animals.

To recognize this as abject cruelty does not entail a naïve romancing of animal life or a quixotic concern for them. We can decry the horrors endured by these animals as abhorrent without putting the animals on the same level as humans or denying the genuine human need to use animals in some circumstances.[7] Therefore, my focus here will not be on the morality of factory farming itself; I will assume that it is morally indefensible. Given the constraints of space, I will also not explore other problems related to meat consumption (its negative environmental impact, the inefficiency of meat as a source of nutrition for a hungry world, the increase of species extinction due to the conversion of forest land for cattle feed, and so forth).[8] The only question I seek to address is whether Christians should, given the cruelty of factory farming and the covenantal status of the animals within it, choose to eat food produced in such an unethical fashion.

I believe it is acceptable for Christians to eat meat. Though Christianity has long valued the practice of meat abstinence, that choice was typically driven more by ascetic interests and a desire to discipline the body than concern for the animals themselves. Nonetheless, compassion for animals was often seen as a sign of saintliness and sometimes a precondition of it. Such compassion is glaringly absent in factory farming and, it would seem, tacitly supported by consumer choice and the quest for cheap meat.

We can eat meat, but can we eat meat produced in this way? A helpful way to begin is to note a distinction made by the Catholic ethical tradition between material cooperation with evil (permitted) and formal cooperation with evil (sinful). The distinction is intended to account for the fact that, sometimes, in order to achieve a good, we must act in ways that support an evil. We live in an imperfect world dominated by structures and systems that are flawed and often sinful. Due to that, as well as human finitude, we will find ourselves in situations where we can't do the good without also doing the evil.

Acts that also advance evil can still be morally good, depending on the agent's intent, the act's proximity to the evil (e.g., did the act directly cause the evil or merely indirectly contribute to it?), and the gravity of the evil. A common example is a politician voting for a bill that has moral flaws but overall advances social justice. In voting for it, the politician cooperates with evil by supporting the bill's moral flaws. Presumably, they would have preferred that the bill be flawless, but unfortunately that was not an option. Acts like these are often matters of material cooperation with evil. In this case, the politician's vote technically supports an evil but not formally (they want and intend only the good, not the evil), and thus their act is not considered sinful. In contrast, a politician who supports the bill precisely because of its moral flaws is engaged in a formal cooperation with that evil, thus making it a sinful choice.

Some argue that eating meat from factory farms is a case of *formal*, not material, cooperation with evil. That is, eating such meat is a sinful act because of the gravity of the evil (the torture imposed on animals) and our tacit cooperation with the evil and indirect support for it. Factory farms are *intentionally* producing cheap meat, and we are *intentionally* choosing to purchase cheap meat. The cheapness of the meat depends *essentially* on a system that disregards animal well-being and prioritizes a brutal efficiency. Thus the cruelty inflicted upon the animals is not a mere side effect of the industry. In factory farms, the suffering endured by the animals and the quest for cheap meat are bound together, and in choosing, intending, one (cheap meat), we are also choosing the other (animal cruelty). By this logic, eating meat from such operations is a type of formal cooperation with evil and thus is a sinful choice.

Additional observations seem to support this verdict. First, factory-farmed animals are fairly advanced creatures both cognitively and socially,[9] features that should be aggressively protected in a Christian, covenantal context. Since the cruelty inflicted on these animals is significant, a high bar is required to justify purchasing factory-farmed meat, something more momentous than, say, the everyday good of social relationships. Second, unlike cases where the evil-cooperating act is an occasional exception to what is otherwise a licit occupation (e.g., the Uber driver who is asked to transport an individual engaged in criminal activity), eating and socializing in an American context *routinely* involves food gained through what virtually all ethicists agree is a morally abhorrent process.

Finally, in the case of eating factory-farmed meat, we have some clarity about the choice confronting us. We are dealing with a state of affairs that, unlike the intricate complexities and intertwined muddles of politics and the economy, has at its heart an evil reality that is easily institutionally demarcated: The meat is or is not produced inhumanely. Unless we've gone through careful effort to buy humanely produced meat, we can be confident that the meat before us was not produced ethically. Cooperating with such an evil practice can be avoided, and therefore, it is argued, should be avoided.

Against these arguments, others maintain that though the treatment of animals on factory farms is unethical and efforts must be made to eschew their products, eating food from such operations is not always sinful but is, in some cases, an instance of *material* cooperation. Extenuating circumstances force difficult choices—for example, preserving the concord of family and friends or participating in a small dinner hosted, at some personal cost, by a socially vulnerable individual. In addition, a number of external and structural factors conspire to make rejecting factory-farmed products difficult (economic pressures, the dominance of "Big Ag," our culture's naïve valorization of technological efficiency, etc.).

Based on these concerns, one could argue for an approach that accepts an in-principle rejection of factory farming and its products while recognizing that commitments to critical human values are sometimes tied to food choices that are not easily or entirely under the agent's control. Our choices in these social contexts are analogous to other sinless acts where unavoidable entanglement in sinful structures—like purchasing clothing that might have been produced in sweatshops—mars an act's intended goodness.

Placing factory-farmed animals in the context of the kingdom, however, introduces additional concerns for Christian consideration. Typical practices in meat production reflect neither the way God values creation nor the Christian task of bringing God's creatures into the liberation of the kingdom. Not all Christians are required to embody kingdom values of harmony and friendship with animals by abstaining from meat, but it does seem important to avoid when possible practices that are so pointedly antithetical to those values and witness to the alternatives. The duty of the entire Christian community is to act before others in ways that edify and build up, even when and perhaps especially when those practices upend and destabilize socially engrained expectations about how we are to relate to nonhuman creatures.

That said, my intent is not finally to argue for one position or the other, at least not here in this brief reflection. Rather, I only suggest, first, that factory farming violates God's hope for the nonhuman world by any objective measure, and, second, that careful discernment is needed before choosing to participate in such scandalous practices.

Finally, in addition to these general considerations, we can recall that the demands of Christian discipleship are not limited to those norms shared by all Christians. God calls each Christian in ways that go beyond those norms, and embracing this calling becomes part of their unique and personal way of following Christ. This personal calling might involve something quite moderate (eating less meat), something radically countercultural (eschewing any violence against animals regardless of personal cost), or something in between. God calls each person to do something but not the same something.

USING ANIMALS IN EXPERIMENTS

The numbers of animals used in the United States for experiments is difficult to determine due to reporting gaps, but estimates range from 30 million to 150 million, with one study suggesting 500 million. Increased use of mice is driving the numbers ever higher.[10] Assessing the ethics of animal experimentation is challenging because—unlike the case of factory farming, an industry that is universally denounced by ethicists—the basic moral facts of animal experiments, particularly the degree to which they are beneficial or indispensable, are more contested. Some argue that "animal research is necessary" and that curtailing such research would have "serious consequences for the health of both humans and animals, both wild and domestic."[11] Others argue that the conclusions drawn from animal research are not "sufficiently reliable as a basis for predicting the effects of drugs, products, and other materials on human beings."[12]

Despite the uncertainty surrounding animal experiments, I think most who are familiar with the specifics would agree that it is not uncommon for them to fall short of accepted ethical norms. Among the more troubling experiments are those that inflict significant pain. Examples include one study that "induced heart failure in dogs by inserting pacemakers that accelerated their hearts to around double the normal rate for up to a month," another that "induced post-traumatic stress disorder in rats by restraining them and exposing them to attempted attacks by a cat for 45-minute periods," and a third that involved "a study of severe lung injury and subcutaneous burning in sheep in which over 40% of their body area was burned with a propane torch and their lungs burned by being forced to inhale hot smoke."[13] The "3Rs" of animal research (*replace* animals with alternatives, *reduce* the number of animals used, and *refine* methods so as to alleviate pain and distress) are widely accepted norms that should prevent the worst cases, but it's unlikely that sufficient regulatory oversight exists to ensure they are followed.

It is not just that animal experiments inflict significant pain on animals. The more noteworthy question that haunts the field is whether the results are reliable and significant enough to justify that pain. Neurologist Aysha Akhtar notes three conditions that explain "why animal experimentation, regardless of the disease category studied, fails to reliably inform human health: (1) the effects of the laboratory environment and other variables on study outcomes, (2) disparities between animal models of disease and human diseases, and (3) species differences in physiology and genetics."[14] Akhtar goes on to list numerous drug trials that were promising when tested on animals but then failed when used on humans. Failures such as these explain the retort by Richard Klausner, former director of the National

Cancer Institute: "The history of cancer research has been a history of curing cancer in the mouse. . . . We have cured mice of cancer for decades—and it simply didn't work in humans."[15]

If true, one might wonder why we continue animal experiments at all. Besides the obvious reason—cases where animal experiments *do* help—two factors encourage continuation. First, the idea of bypassing animals and immediately testing unproven drugs and procedures on humans raises the haunting specter of past abuses that the use of animals is supposed to prevent (recall the infamous Tuskegee experiments). Even if the predictive quality of animal experiments is marginal, it has the social benefit of avoiding the disturbing scenario of using human subjects as the first step in testing drugs and medical protocols. Second, forms of institutional inertia—caused by funding structures, academic credentialing, investment preferences, and bio-industrial interests (e.g., marketing of genetically engineered mice)—foster uncritical support for experimental practices.

It is impossible to adequately address all the issues at stake here. Instead, I will focus on the in-principle question: Are animal experiments ever justified from a Christian perspective, and, if so, why? Given the scope and severity of the harms caused to animals, an ethical analysis of animal experiments, more than any other use of animals, requires that we first clarify our understanding of what exactly we believe the role and value of animal life to be.

A Catholic view, guided by pre-Vatican II attitudes, might say that an animal's value lies exclusively in its capacity to serve human need. If that's our starting point, then the bar for what constitutes ethical behavior when experimenting on animals is set relatively low. Since God created animals with the exclusive purpose of serving humanity, the argument would go, then even those experiments that entail severe suffering and death pose no conflict with their divinely intended purpose. The animal's "end," the reason why it was created, is being respected.

This narrowly anthropocentric approach—what Francis calls a "tyrannical anthropocentrism"—is generally criticized in contemporary Catholic thought. As an alternative approach, I understand the ultimate end of animals as that of sharing in a relationship with God within the harmonious life of the kingdom. Placing animals in this eschatological context limits anthropocentric claims: Though animals may be used to advance human need, that is not their ultimate end or the purpose for which they were created. Framing experiments within the perspective of the kingdom does not lead us to reject such practices, but it does require critical investigations of whether and when they are genuinely needed. The default norm, as instructed by the values of the kingdom, is that animal experiments are wrong; they do not reflect what God ultimately intends for that creature.

Nonetheless many medical experiments on animals seem justified at the present time, in a world that is still awaiting its final liberation. The standard for justifying these experiments in the eschatological framework I'm presenting is, however, something stricter than a vague appeal to "reasonable limits." Pressing human need and the well-founded expectation of redressing that need, assessed within the context of an empathetic concern for animal well-being, are more fitting standards for an activity so contrary to the covenantal end that has been established for all creatures in Christ.

Short of forgoing all medical treatment, individual Christians cannot realistically make the unilateral choice to avoid the benefits of animal experiments. Medical care depends on an interconnected web of historical experiments and investigations that cannot be untangled so as to allow even the most committed activist to choose only those medical procedures, therapies, and drugs that result exclusively from ethical research. The *communal* witness of the Church, however, serves an important role here because the attitudes and assumptions underlying support for animal experiments (attitudes and assumptions to which Christian beliefs have historically contributed) are socially legitimatized and not merely the punctuated expression of individual sin. The Church's rejection of what Pope Francis calls the "technocratic paradigm"—the naïve hope that technology can solve all our problems without any need for humanity to change and grow in virtue—can help raise social awareness about the untested and unreflective assumptions operating in our society's moral intuitions and help reform them to be more critically conscious of animal welfare.

In its ecclesial witness, the Christian community (as individuals and as a collective voice) should share with the world its distinctive vision of animal life. This vision is shaped by the good of relationality. As noted in chapter 2, we have become aware of the rich interior lives of animals and the complexity of their social relationships, and we can imagine, given God's covenantal plans, that God highly values and desires these qualities. Animals can be in relation with us because they are "subjects," creatures that act and, through those actions, relate to other creatures. Valuing an animal's subjectivity, however, also requires that we recognize its interests as a subject—that is, the animal's desire to live a life free of pain, fear, and desperate need.

The animal's subjecthood merits particular attention because it is the property that is most severely and directly threatened by a technocratic instrumentalization. All forms of animal use (whether as food sources, beasts of burden, or objects of enjoyment and sport) entail an element of animal instrumentalization in which the animal is viewed as *merely* an object or instrument to serve human interest. However, using animals in experiments is distinctively instrumentalizing in that it effectively eliminates any other frame of reference for relating to the animal beyond that of a tool for human need. The erasure of the animal's subjectivity is required for animal research, and, correspondingly, any natural empathy one might feel for animals as sentient subjects must be suppressed and any sense of each animal's individuality expunged, so that they can be transformed into generic caches of data.[16]

Christianity's interest in opposing this purging of creaturely subjecthood is grounded in what it sees as the animal's end and purpose (life with God in the kingdom) and its responsibility to serve that end. The biologically odd appearance of sentience in evolutionary history—odd in that we still understand so little about how and why it emerged—is a revolutionary event for God's goal of establishing a covenantal relationship with creation. We do not genuinely *see* animals—see what God has made them to be—when we treat them *merely* as objects and not as sentient subjects.

As a way of helping us recalibrate how we think about animal experimentation, we can consider the thought experiment offered by the Christian ethicist Donna Yarri. She proposes prohibiting "any kind of pain and suffering to experimental animals to which a pet owner would be unwilling to expose her own pet."[17] Imagining such a scenario elicits moral passions attuned to the distinctive identity of a nonhuman animal more effectively than abstract thinking about it. I recognize that most would view this standard as unrealistic, but perhaps that is the point: to do what Jesus's parables did, upending conventional ways of viewing the world and disrupting whatever complacency or self-deception is at play. The thought experiment reminds us that laboratory animals are, in every morally relevant way, similar to the companion animals that share our homes; in both cases we are dealing with nonhuman, creaturely subjects with individual personalities, developed cognition, and a desire for their own distinctive forms of flourishing.

Though one might conclude from the above that animal experiments should always be opposed as inherently wrong, that is not what I am proposing. The advancement of science and medicine is an important good to be praised; it serves the worthy endeavor of liberating our world from the natural evils that plague it. Sometimes that effort will entail difficult choices between the good of human creatures and that of nonhuman creatures, choices that are to be avoided when possible and mourned when not.

CONCLUSION

Faced with the end of his own life, the whisky priest of Graham Greene's *The Power and the Glory* reflected, "It was too easy to die for what was good or beautiful"; we need "a God to die for the half-hearted and the corrupt." Christ's saving message was radical partly because it was *not* directed toward the beautiful and powerful of the world but the scorned and sinful: "I did not come to call the righteous but sinners" (Matthew 9:13). The Christian is called to make this same swerve in their treatment of their fellow humans—to devote distinctive care and concern to the poor, the powerless, and the scorned because such was Jesus's example. This is the Christian's way of witnessing to the kingdom of God and "to be, on earth, the initial budding of that kingdom" (*Lumen Gentium*, §5).

But the kingdom's swerve is not just for relations with our fellow humans. If our hope is that animals are to join us in the kingdom of God, then it would seem that our responses to them should be informed by the ideals of the kingdom and God's desire for relationships with them. This is not the official framework used by the Church, though much of what Pope Francis says about animals aligns with it. Encouraging relationships with animals that conform to the peaceable kingdom, the pope praises his namesake Francis of Assisi for his conviction that "each and every creature was a sister united to him by bonds of affection. That is why he felt called to care for all that exists." The pope knows that such a saintly attitude toward animals will be "written off as naive romanticism." However, he maintains that is a perilous dismissal. For if we "no longer speak the language of fraternity and beauty in our relationship with the world, our attitude will be that of masters, consumers, ruthless exploiters, unable to set limits on their immediate needs. By contrast, if we feel intimately united with all that exists, then sobriety and care will well up spontaneously" (*Laudato Si'*, §11).

If God's ultimate hope and desire for the individual animals of our present age is that they come to enjoy a world where they will know only the harmony and compassion of the kingdom, it seems reasonable to suppose that God would want those whom he has appointed stewards to begin fashioning such a world. It is, of course, beyond human ability to liberate creation from its present travails. Nonetheless, the Christian community can, without "the excuse of realism and pragmatism" (*Laudato Si'*, §217), strive to embody God's eschatological hope for creation and its animals whenever and however grace allows it to do so.

NOTES

1. For an overview of the history of factory farming, see Michael Pollan, *The Omnivore's Dilemma: A Natural History of Four Meals* (New York: Penguin, 2007).
2. Hal Herzog, *Some We Love, Some We Hate, Some We Eat: Why It's So Hard to Think Straight about Animals* (New York: Harper, 2010), 167–68.
3. Herzog, 168.
4. Joseph Ratzinger, *God and the World: A Conversation with Peter Seewald* (San Francisco: Ignatius Press, 2002), 78–79, emphasis added.
5. Gail A. Eisnitz, *Slaughterhouse: The Shocking Story of Greed, Neglect, and Inhumane Treatment Inside the U.S. Meat Industry* (Amherst, NY: Prometheus Books, 2007), 87–88.
6. "Abstract," Amy J. Fitzgerald, Linda Kalof, and Thomas Dietz, "Slaughterhouses and Increased Crime Rates: An Empirical Analysis of the Spillover from 'The Jungle' into the Surrounding Community," *Organization & Environment* 22, no. 2 (2009): 158.
7. Christopher Belshaw, "Meat," in *The Moral Complexities of Eating Meat*, ed. Ben Bramble and Bob Fischer (New York: Oxford University Press, 2015), 9–29.
8. For an introduction to the mass extinction underway, see Elizabeth Kolbert, *The Sixth Extinction: An Unnatural History* (New York: Henry Holt and Company, 2014). Some of the other issues are explored in Martin C. Parlasca and Matin Qaim, "Meat Consumption and Sustainability," *Annual Review of Resource Economics* 14 (2022).
9. Barry Estabrook offers an account of the cognitive qualities of pigs and the suffering they endure in factory farming. Pigs are, he shows, extremely social and playful creatures, with an intelligence and conscious awareness at least as developed as that of dogs. Barry Estabrook, *Pig Tales: An Omnivore's Quest for Sustainable Meat* (New York: W.W. Norton & Company, 2015).
10. David Clough, *On Animals*, vol. 2, *Theological Ethics* (London: T&T Clark, 2019), 132.
11. A. K. Kiani et al., "Ethical considerations regarding animal experimentation," *Journal of Preventive Medicine and Hygiene* 63, no. 2, suppl. 3 (2022).
12. David DeGrazia and Tom L. Beauchamp, "Guest Editorial: Reassessing Animal Research Ethics," *Cambridge Quarterly of Healthcare Ethics* 24, no. 4 (2015): 385. For a comprehensive critique of animal experiments, see Andrew Linzey and Clair Linzey, eds., *The Ethical Case against Animal Experiments* (Urbana, IL: University of Illinois Press, 2018).
13. Clough, *On Animals*, 136. He cites an article by H. P. Ferdowsian and J. P. Gluck, "The Ethical Challenge of Animal Research," *Cambridge Quarterly of Health Care Ethics* 24, no. 4 (2015): 394.
14. Aysha Akhtar, "The Flaws and Human Harms of Animal Experimentation," *Cambridge Quarterly of Health Care Ethics* 24, no. 4 (2015): 408.
15. Marlene Cimons, Josh Getlin, and Thomas H. Maugh II, "Cancer Drugs Face Long Road from Mice to Men," *Los Angeles Times*, May 6, 1998.
16. For a secular version of this concern, see Silvia Caprioglio Panizza, "The Reification of Non-Human Animals," *Cambridge Quarterly of Health Care Ethics* 32, no. 1 (2023): 90–104.
17. Donna Yarri, *The Ethics of Animal Experimentation: A Critical Analysis and Constructive Christian Proposal* (New York, Oxford: Oxford University Press, 2005), 102.

FURTHER READING

Most of the sources for this chapter's discussions can be found in chapter 5 of *All God's Animals: A Catholic Theological Framework for Animal Ethics*. Washington, DC: Georgetown University Press, 2019, 190–207.

Cases in Animal Ethics: Meat Eating and Animal Experiments

Imhoff, Dan. *The CAFO Reader: The Tragedy of Industrial Animal Factories*. Healdsburg, CA; Berkeley, CA: Watershed Media, 2010.

Regan, Tom, ed. *Animal Sacrifices: Religious Perspectives on the Use of Animals in Science*. Philadelphia: Temple University Press, 1986.

Yarri, Donna. *The Ethics of Animal Experimentation: A Critical Analysis and Constructive Christian Proposal*. New York: Oxford University Press, 2005.

Zaraska, Marta. "Meet the Meat Paradox." *Scientific American*. July 1, 2016.

POSTSCRIPT

The Ambassador Dog

A heartwarming video praising dogs has circulated the internet for over a decade. It begins: "And on the ninth day, God looked down on his wide-eyed children and said they need a companion. So, God made a Dog." The video goes on to list other reasons for God's decision to create a dog:

> God said I need somebody to wake up and give kisses. . . . I need somebody willing to sit, then stay, then roll over then with no ego or complaint dress in hats they do not need and costumes they do not understand. . . . Somebody no matter what you didn't do, or couldn't take, or didn't win, or couldn't make will love you without judgment just the same. So God made a Dog.[1]

God made the dog with a task in mind: to give joy to their human companions and help them feel loveworthy, especially when the world says otherwise.

If I were to take the video more seriously than I should, with its idea that God made dogs for some providential reason, I'd wonder if God might have an additional goal in mind. God knew that we'd tend to focus on ourselves and our immediate surroundings and, as a result, we'd miss all the delightful things bursting forth in the natural world. Perhaps God decided to fashion some creature to remind humanity of those wonders. This creature would have to be special, a creature with two paws in the animal world and two paws comfortably in the domain of humans. God would use the animal's distinct form of goodness to draw our attention to the natural world and help us cherish it as God does. The creature would effectively be God's ambassador for the nonhuman world. St. Augustine found divine providence at work in all aspects of his life; maybe we can allow ourselves to do the same with our canine companions. So God made a dog.

Dogs *are* special. They have a natural ability to interpret our facial expressions and read our bodies' subtle emotional cues. Because of this skill, dogs make great companion animals for people with various needs, including those on the spectrum. Dogs are also good for our hearts and relieving stress. Simply petting a dog lowers blood pressure. They help with our social lives too: A couple of studies suggest that men are more likely to have dating success when they're accompanied by a dog. Probably their biggest claim to fame, besides their loyalty to humans, is their superpower sense of smell—by some estimates 100,000 times more powerful than ours. They can detect a teaspoon of sugar in a million gallons of water, almost two Olympic-sized pools. To put it in other terms: If we took *one* grain of sugar and somehow managed to divide it into 50 equal parts (!), then put one of those parts (1/50th of a grain of sugar) into a gallon of water, our dogs would be able to notice.

But dogs are not the only special creatures. God's amazing creation is filled with stunning delights. In the perennial contest between cat and dog lovers about which species is superior, cats win the facial expression category hands down. The performance of dogs is passably mediocre. Estimates suggest they have twenty to thirty unique expressions, many depending on the position of their ears, while cats, according to one study, have close to three hundred. Confirming the unfairness of the natural world, roosters aren't bothered by their crowing as they have built-in earplugs. The average NBA player can jump about 28 inches, with the record being four feet, a thoroughly unimpressive feat compared to pumas who can vertically jump fifteen feet from a standing position. Hummingbirds are avian acrobats. They are the only birds that can hover and fly backward, sideways, and upside down. Those accomplishments are made possible by a skeleton structure that allows the birds to flap their wings, over fifty times a second, in a figure-eight shape instead of just up and down like other birds. Were they to need IDs, reindeers would have their eye color listed as "depends on the season." Their eyes transform from yellow in the summer to blue in the winter. Their winter blues are over a thousand times more sensitive to light than their summer yellows. In battles sure to delight puerile humor enthusiasts everywhere, lemurs hold stink competitions as a way to resolve conflicts without physical fights. Sea cucumbers are natural shapeshifters due to their unique collagen tissue (the material that forms bones and ligaments); unlike the tissue in humans, the stiffness of a sea cucumber's collagen is mutable,

able to change from hard to jelly-like depending on whatever their nervous system decides is needed at the time.

Dogs are amazing, but not uniquely so. Still, they *are* relatively distinct in the special relationship they have with humanity, and perhaps one could imagine God saving dogs but not the rest of the animal world. That's not the direction I've taken in this book. Though a dog-lover myself, I have avoided arguments that dogs or any companion animals are in heaven simply because of their relationships with humans or, worse in my mind, simply because of our felt need for them to be there. It's not about us but about God's plan in Jesus Christ.

My approach has been to argue that animals are in heaven because God includes them in the salvific work of Christ. The issue, then, of whether dogs or other companion animals are in heaven is only one part of a broader question of what God has planned for *all* the animals of the world. I want to defend the hope that God's plan is to save them, bringing them home to him, pets and nonpets alike, and to do so in Christ Jesus and with humanity. My arguments do not prove that animals will join us in heaven (that's for God to decide and the Church to discern), but they do amply justify a hope for that inclusion based on sound theological reasons.

Those reasons are plentiful, and their strength lies not just in their numbers but also in the different angles and perspectives they bring to the issue. I argued, for example, that Aquinas's reasoning excludes too many animals; some animals can meet a version of the bar that Aquinas set for the transition to the next life without threatening human distinctiveness. Like many animal lovers, I'm heartened by the inclusion of animals in Old Testament depictions of the age to come (e.g., Isaiah 11). Still, I don't believe those as significant as other biblical and magisterial testimonies. A variety of sources, for example, maintain that a common fate links the destiny of animals to that of humanity: the speeches and images of Old Testament prophets; the shared woundedness that humanity's sin caused to both humanity and animals; Romans 8, which ties creation's liberation to the children of God; and the arguments of St. John Chrysostom. Also, God's offer of the covenant, so central to Old Testament theology, includes animals on at least two occasions. Pope Francis's emphasis on the relationality of all creatures and on God's intent to be in relationship with them continues that covenantal theme in a new register. Early doctors of the Church—Irenaeus, Chrysostom, Athanasius, Ephrem—believed creation would be saved because revelation taught them as much. A few of them developed theologies of creation's salvation based on the cosmic Christ theme of Ephesians and Colossians; God's plan for creation is to sum up all things in Christ. According to recent popes, we pray for, and give ritual expression to, such an end at Mass, as is particularly evident in the Fourth Eucharistic Prayer.

Our common evolutionary heritage with animals and scientific insights into the cognitive sophistication of animals give a different kind of support for an animal-inclusive salvation: They raise questions about the absolute distinction traditionally drawn between human and nonhuman animals and, in turn, render suspect the humans-only theories of salvation built on that distinction. Similarly, the theodicy of innocent animal suffering haunts attempts to preserve a humans-only resurrection: It is difficult to defend God's goodness if the end of a pig's life is eternal oblivion after a lifetime of warehouse torture. That pig's life needs a next chapter, an afterlife, so that its story doesn't end with the hell of its present life.

Additional support comes from Vatican II's embrace of a cosmic eschatology, which maintains that the salvific work of Christ, somehow, encompasses all creation. This cosmic scope is fully supported in the writings of John Paul II and Benedict and further developed in Francis's *Laudato Si'*. Humanity has a role to play in this cosmic salvation. In the Church's more creation-friendly interpretations of humanity as the *imago Dei* and of the dominion mandate of Genesis, humanity is meant to shepherd creation for God's sake, not just use it. This understanding provides a helpful correction to what Francis has called tyrannical anthropocentrism and a basis for his view that God created animals for his divine pleasure, not just because of human need.

Laudato Si' has rightly drawn our attention to God's care for the concrete, individual animal. Based on that, I've suggested that the Church's belief in creation's salvation is best understood as one addressed to the individual creature in ways appropriate to that creature. This allows for the possibility that God's salvation will not take the same form for all animals. Perhaps it will (resurrection for each and every creature?), but it seems reasonable that it will vary depending on the animal. God may, we can hope, resurrect creatures with developed subjectivity and consciousness (crows and chimpanzees) but offer a different type of restoration or re-creation for less cognitively sophisticated creatures (ticks and worms).

I also argued that this salvific care for the individual creature has another implication: It shows the deficiency of salvation by proxy. Preserving an individual creature's sentience through its resurrection is the only way God can genuinely save a sentient creature. Other forms of salvation might restore or replicate the creature's *body*, but lost forever would be its unique subjectivity and consciousness—that which gives the creature its particular identity. The idea that God would save such creatures through some sort of proxy representation of them is at odds with the emphasis in Francis's encyclical on God's salvific care for concrete, individual animals.

Against detractors who believe the idea of animals being saved and joining us in heaven is absurd, I sketched a theology of animals to show why and how the idea makes sense. In keeping with a theory of animal salvation grounded in the relational life of the Trinity, I imagined a heaven for animals in which they would continue their participation in the divine life, bonded with Christ and each other through the Spirit, in a vast heavenly ecosystem of eternal interchange and play.

If God cares enough about all the creatures he's made to save them in Christ, then we need to re-hone our moral instincts about animals in light of that divine interest. I approach this ethical attunement through the lens of the kingdom of God. The proclamation of the kingdom was central to Jesus's teaching, and since Vatican II, the Church has understood witnessing to that kingdom—"to be, on earth, the initial budding forth of that kingdom" (*Lumen Gentium*, §5)—as part of its identity. The natural world will be part of the kingdom, and thus our relationships with it in the present age should anticipate life in the kingdom in whatever way circumstances and God's grace allow us to do.

Appealing to the teachings of the first chapters of Genesis, Pope Francis states that "human life is grounded in three fundamental and closely intertwined relationships: with God, with our neighbour and with the earth itself" (*LS*, §66). Or, at least, our lives should be so grounded. Sin has, unfortunately, ruptured "these three vital relationships." As followers of Christ, it is our responsibility to work to undo the damage of sin and restore those relationships. The first step in "healing [sin's] rupture" is, Francis suggests, establishing "the harmony which Saint Francis of Assisi experienced with all creatures" (*LS*, §66).

What Francis has in mind is more than additional environmental practices; such harmony requires a new and renewed affection for the natural world, what Francis calls a "profound interior conversion" (*LS*, §21) and John Paul described as an "ecological conversion." Maybe our attending to the witness of animals can foster this conversion of heart and mind—a possibility raised in Job's exhortation that we learn from the creatures of the world:

> But now ask the beasts to teach you,
> the birds of the air to tell you;
> Or speak to the earth to instruct you,
> and the fish of the sea to inform you.
> Which of all these does not know
> that the hand of God has done this?
> (Job 12:7–9)

Job reminds us that if we attend to our world carefully—observe it not merely with a peek and a gander but study it deeply, prayerfully—we'll find ourselves drawn by the sacred. Graced looking shows the otherwise spiritually stolid, biotic shapes surrounding us as lives shimmering with the transcendent, sacramental intimations of the God who created them.

Perhaps then we can allow our imagination to go wild for a moment and wonder if God might use our fanciful canine ambassadors as guides to help us in the ecological conversion commended by John Paul and Francis. After all, God has given each of us a role in helping the kingdom grow; maybe he also has a mission for dogs, some providential plan for them to serve the kingdom. And maybe it's a mission that draws us together in the mutuality God so loves. We, as stewards of God's creation, serve dogs as caretakers, while dogs serve us by helping us grow in that stewardship and teaching us what it means to have compassionate care for God's animals. Following this imaginary logic, God didn't send canine animals simply for our joy, but for our instruction. They are our teachers in the school of animal kindness. If that is the case, loving dogs is just the first step in learning Christlike care for animals, not its end point.

And so, God made a dog.

NOTE

1. "God Made a Dog," https://www.youtube.com/watch?v=9wWHLdHroyQ. The creation of the dog takes place on the ninth day, not the eighth, in deference to a video narrated by Paul Harvey. That video, made famous at the 2013 Super Bowl, began, "And on the eighth day, God made a farmer." The dog-creation video intentionally mimics the cadence and style of that earlier video.

INDEX

abstract thought, 14, 16
abuse, of animals, 20, 29, 139. *See also* suffering
Acta Sanctorum, 37, 41n17
activism, 155
agency: of animals, 100; God's will and, 139; reflexive moral, 36; Trinity and, 93
All God's Animals: A Catholic Theological Framework for Animal Ethics (Steck), 2
"already / not yet" perspective, 135–38
amoebas, 108
angels, 105, 110
Anglicans, 20–21
animal rights ethics, 129
animals: abuse of, 20, 139; in Aquinas, 12–15; Bible on, 47–63; bodies of, 14; in Boullier, 30–31; in *Catechism of the Catholic Church,* 78–81; Catholic ethics and, 132; Catholic theology of, 144–45; Catholic tradition on, 9–26; Catholic views of, in modern period, 20–24; for clothing, 80; companion, 5, 10–12, 73, 81; conflicts with, 135–38; covenant and, 53–55; as cruel to each other, 31, 113; cruelty toward, 20–21, 24, 29–30, 132; in Descartes, 29–30; domestication of, 136; dominion over, 50–51, 79; enmity with, 135–38; in Eucharistic Prayers, 96–97; experimentation in, 148, 153–56; extinction of, 28; Fall and, 47, 51–53, 105, 107; feast of St. Anthony the Abbot and, 99; in Ficino, 20; as food for each other, 113, 126–27; as food for humans, 47, 80, 148–52; friendships between, 34–35; God as loving, 20; as God's creatures *vs.* that of humans, 38; God's plan for, 55–61; goodness of, 73–74; grace and, 111–12; as having duty to humans, 1, 15, 20–24, 39; as having individual unique qualities, 73; human duty to, 21–22; human love for, 73; human role in salvation of, 96; humans as, 31–32; individuality of, 77; interior life of, 34; magisterial teachings on, between Vatican II and *Laudato Si',* 69–70; in Manning, 38; in minority tradition, 36–39; moral duty to, 132; and nature *vs.* grace, 106–7; personalities of, 73–74; personhood of, 17–18; play by, 113; preference for some, over others, 143; principle of common fate and, 59–60; relationships among, 34–35, 74, 113–14; relationships of, with God, 112–13; research on, 153–54; resurrection of, 70–71, 77–78, 104; in Ruland, 39; salvation of, 48, 57–58, 62–63, 66–82; science and, 32–36; sociality among, 34–35; souls of, 13; as subjectively aware, 17; suffering of, 29–31, 80, 148; as term, 5; theodicy of, 29–32;

animals (*continued*)
unpleasant, 108; vivisection of, 21–22; in wilderness, 136–37; as "work of Christ," 2. *See also specific organisms*
animal welfare, 21, 23, 148, 155
Anthony of Padua, 37
Anthony the Abbot, 99
anthropocentrism, 58, 62, 78–79, 137, 154, 164
anthropomorphism, 33–34, 39, 73
apostolic constitutions, 75
Apostolic Constitutions, 97
appropriation, 92–93
Aquinas, Thomas: on animals, 12–15; arguments of, against animals in heaven, 15; Fall in, 51–52; indirect love of animals in, 132; instinct in, 95; on love of animals, 132; moral duty in, 132; overview of thought, 12–13; reason in, 12–13, 19, 24; resurrection in, 13, 17, 19, 24; soul in, 13–14; updating approach of, to animals, 16–19. *See also* Thomists
Aristotle, 13, 18, 131
Arnauld, Antoine, 30
Athanasius of Alexandria, 37, 163
Augustine, 90, 108, 162
authoritativeness, 4–5

Bacon, Francis, 20
bacteria, 108
Balthasar, Hans Urs von, 88–92, 94–95, 100, 101n2
Bartholomew, Patriarch, 6
beatific vision, 15, 87, 104, 109–11
behavior: heaven as reward for, 108; predatory, 114–15; in stimulus-response framework, 33
Bellarmine, Robert, 1
Benedict XII, Pope, 109
Benedict XV, Pope, 38
Benedict XVI, Pope, 1, 29, 37, 69–70, 89, 98, 109. *See also* Ratzinger, Joseph
Bergoglio, Jorge, 66. *See also* Francis, Pope
birds, 34, 50, 55, 149, 162
body(ies): of animals, 14; of Christ, 98; in composite of person, 13; in death, 14–16; in Descartes, 30; in heaven, 17, 104; in mirror test, 34; resurrection and, 15, 109–10; soul and, 13
bonobos, 33–34
Book of Blessings (US Conference of Catholic Bishops), 99
Bougeant, Guillaume-Hyacinthe, 31
Boullier, David, 30–31
Boyle, Robert, 21
Bunyan, John, 111

calling, 138–39
Caritas in Veritate (Benedict XVI), 69
Catechism of the Catholic Church, 4, 11, 38; animals in, 78–81, 95; animal suffering in, 80, 132; creation in, 51, 58; heaven in, 109–10, 112, 116; kingdom of God in, 68; soul in, 15
Cathedral of Santa Maria Assunta (Torcello), 104
cats, 162
charity, 22, 38, 132
chickens, 126–27, 149
chimpanzees, 33–34
clothing, animals for, 80
Cobbe, Frances Power, 21
cock fighting, 126–27
cognition, 3, 16, 19; salvation and, 71–73; subjectivity and, 74
Colossians, Letter to, 36, 59–60, 63
communion, 11, 49–50, 62, 117
"Communion and Stewardship" (International Theological Commission), 49–50

companion animals, 5, 10–12, 73, 81. *See also* cats; dogs; pets
compassion, saintly, 1
Congregation for the Doctrine of the Faith (CDF), 4, 18–19, 49
connectedness, 76
consciousness, 5, 16–19, 24, 34, 74, 129, 164
continuity, 16–19
conversion, ecological, 69, 165–66
Corinthians, First Book of, 62
Corinthians, Second Book of, 57, 91
Council of Nicaea, 67
covenant, 48, 53–55, 60, 69, 74–77, 111–12, 144, 150, 155–56, 163
creation: in Benedict XVI, 69; Christ as end point of, 36, 59; eschatology and, 61; Eucharist and, 97; Eucharistic Prayers and, 97–98; in Francis, 76; Holy Spirit and, 69; humanity as microcosm of, 71–72; humanity as responsible for, 48–50; *imago Dei* and, 49; in John Paul II, 69–70; new, 57–58, 68; praying for, 139; preserving integrity of, 18, 105–6; principle of common fate and, 59–60; redemption and, 73; relationships and, 76; replacement salvation and, 71; respect for integrity of, 79; salvation and, 143; stewardship of, 50, 138; as work of Christ, 2
creatures: charity toward, 38; communion with, 11; defined, 5; as having souls, 13; less-developed, 16, 144; trinitarianism and, 88. *See also* animals
Crousaz, Jean Pierre de, 31
crows, 34, 113–14
cruelty: of animals toward animals, 31; in ethics, 132; moral duty to avoid, 132; toward animals, 20–21, 24, 29–30
culling, 148

Daniel, Book of, 95
Dante Alighieri, 111
Darwin, Charles, 31
death: of Christ, 90, 92, 100; Fall and, 51; goodness and, 74; mourning of, by animals, 35; resurrection and, 109–10; salvation and, 72–73; sentience and, 18; sin and, 37
deontology, 127–29
Descartes, René, 29–30
Dicastery for the Doctrine of the Faith, 4
Dickey, James, 115–16
dignity, 80, 132
divine economy, 2
dogs, 9–10, 17, 23, 115, 143, 158n9, 161–64, 166n1
dolphins, 34
domestication, 136. *See also* factory farming; pets
Domininum et Vivificantem (John Paul II), 52, 70
dominion, 47, 50–51, 69, 79–81, 138, 145–47, 164
Dumbo (films), 125

Easter, 100
Ecclesia de Eucharista (John Paul II), 98
ecological conversion, 69, 165–66
ecology, 66, 69. *See also* environmental crisis
elephants, 34–35
encyclicals, 75
enmity, with animals, 135–38
environmental concerns, 27–29, 61, 68–70, 165. *See also* ecology
Ephesians, Letter to, 2, 36, 59–60, 63
Ephrem the Syrian, 37, 59, 163
eschatology: cosmic, 3, 40, 67–68, 98, 164; creation and, 61; defined, 67; principle of common fate and, 60; Second Vatican Council and, 82n1
Estabrook, Barry, 158n9

ethics: "already / not yet" perspective and, 135–38; of animal experimentation, 153–56; animal farming and, 126–27; animal rights, 129; applied, 143–57; Catholic, 129–32; in deontology, 128; in early views of animals, 22; kingdom of God and, 132–35; of meat-eating, 148–52; natural law in, 130–31; philosophical approaches to animal, 126–29; principles in, 144–48; theory in, 125–40; in utilitarianism, 127–28; values and, 133–34; virtue, 127, 130–32, 149. *See also* vivisection
Eucharist, 70, 96–98, 101
Eucharistic Prayers, 96–98, 108, 164
evil: cooperation with, 150–52; goodness and, 106; meat-eating and, 150–51; in natural law, 130; in utilitarianism, 128
evolution, 31–32, 52, 164
Exodus, Book of, 53
experimentation, on animals, 148, 153–56. *See also* vivisection
extinction, 28, 76, 117–18, 150
Ezekiel, Book of, 57, 60

Fall, the, 47, 51–53, 61, 105, 107, 130
farming, factory, 126–27, 143, 148–52
fate, principle of common, 59–60
Father, the, 89–93, 100. *See also* God
Federal Emergency Management Agency (FEMA), 11
Ficino, Marsilio, 20
Fidei Depositum (John Paul II), 4
flood, 37, 53–54, 60
food, animals as, 47, 80, 113, 126–27, 148–52
forgiveness, 134
Foundations of Morality: God; Man; Lower Creatures (Ruland), 39
Francis, Pope, 1, 29, 38; on communion with animals, 11; cosmic eschatology in, 164; creation in, 76; God's love in, 55; on Holy Spirit, 93; *Laudato Si'*, 4–5, 11, 15, 48, 51–52, 55, 66, 75–78, 88, 95–96, 157, 164; original sin in, 52; on prayer, 6; relationships in, 165; resurrection in, 77–78; salvation in, 75–78; stewardship in, 50–51; trinitarianism in, 88. *See also* Bergoglio, Jorge
Francis of Assisi, 37, 66, 79, 99
friendship, between animals, 34–35, 114. *See also* relationships
functional approach, 49

Gaudium et Spes (Second Vatican Council), 27–28, 111–12
Genesis, Book of, 47–54, 60, 62, 107, 113, 135, 165
goats, 114, 117
God: animal relationships with, 112–13; animals as creatures of, *vs.* that of humans, 38; animal theodicy and, 29–32; calling of persons by, to actions, 139; covenant and, 53–55; as Father, 89–93, 100; as Holy Spirit, 89; *imago Dei*, 48–50, 101n1; importance of relationality for, 145; interdependence and, 116; kingdom of, 4, 54, 62, 68, 110, 116, 132–38, 144; as loving animals, 20, 55; plan of, for animals, 55–61; in relational approach, 49; relationships as intended by, 76; revelation of, 89–90; salvation and, 2; sin and relationship to humanity of, 91–92; as Son, 89–93, 100, 144; Trinity and, 88, 93–94; will of, agency and, 139. *See also* Father, the
goodness, 73–74, 106
gorillas, 33–34
grace, 38, 92, 105–7, 111–12, 138
Great Divorce, The (Lewis), 111
Greene, Graham, 157
grieving, 35

healing: animal suffering in advance of human, 148, 153, 155; grace and, 107
health, animal suffering in advance of human, 148, 153, 155
heaven: animals in, 104–18; beatific vision and, 15, 104, 109–10; body in, 17, 104; in *Catechism of the Catholic Church,* 109–10; depictions of, 111; earth as foreshadowing of, 112; environmental concerns and, 68; Eucharist and, 98; in Isaiah, 57; life in, 15; in *Lumen Gentium,* 67; new, 57–58; in Revelation, 57; as reward, 108; in Second Vatican Council, 112
"Heaven of Animals, The" (Dickey), 115–16
Hebrews, Book of, 54
Herzog, Hal, 126–27
"Historical Roots of Our Ecologic Crisis, The" (White), 27
Holy Spirit, 2, 58, 61, 68–69, 89, 92–96, 98, 100, 112. *See also* God
Hosea, Book of, 55, 60, 62
human nature, 92–93, 105–6
human/nonhuman binary, 32, 146
humans: as animals, 31–32; animals as having duty to, 1, 15, 20–24, 39; communion and, 49–50; dominion of, 47; in Fall, 47, 51–53; in functional approach, 49; as having dominion over animals, 50–51; as having duty to animals, 21–22; *imago Dei* and, 48–50; immortality of souls of, 14–15; in *Laudato Si',* 75–76; as microcosm of creation, 71–72; need for relationships of, 76; pleasure of, at expense of animals, 148; principle of common fate and, 59–60; redemption of, 37; in relational approach, 49; in salvation, 96; sin and God's relationship to, 91–92; souls of, *vs.* animals, 13; as stewards, 49–50, 69, 79
Hummes, Claudio, 66
Hurricane Katrina, 10–11

idolatry, 10
Ignatius of Loyola, 139
imago Dei, 48–50, 101n1
immortality, of soul, 13–15
Incarnation, 90–91
individuality, of creatures, 77
insects, 1, 16, 24, 33, 72, 82
instinct, 95
instrumentalization, 155–56
intelligence, 22, 33, 50, 158n9
interconnectedness, 76
interdependence, 116
interior life, of animals, 34
International Theological Commission (ITC), 4–5, 19, 49, 109
Irenaeus of Lyons, 36, 59, 97, 163
Isaiah, Book of, 57, 60, 62, 113, 163
ITC (International Theological Commission), 4–5, 19, 49, 109

Jeremiah, Book of, 53–54
Jesus Christ: appropriation and, 92–93; body of, 98; covenant and, 53–54; creation and, 36, 59; as end point of creation, 36; Eucharist and, 97; in Eucharistic Prayers, 98; "liquefication" of, 94, 100; love of animals by, 38–39; in relational approach, 49; relationship with, salvation and, 111; resurrection of, 73, 97, 113; sacrifice of, 73; salvation and, 2, 59, 68, 90–92, 94; Second Coming of, 4, 67, 110, 133; as summing up all things, 2; Trinity and, 90–92, 95; values of, 133–34; work of, 2
Job, Book of, 55, 59, 165–66
John, Gospel of, 104, 133

John Chrysostom, 37, 39, 52, 70, 163
John Paul II, Pope, 1, 22, 29; animal experimentation in, 148; Balthasar and, 88–89; covenant in, 53; creation in, 69–70; *Domininum et Vivificantem,* 52, 70; *Ecclesia de Eucharista,* 98; environmentalism in, 69–70; on Eucharist, 98; *Evangelium Vitae,* 51; *Fidei Depositum,* 4; new creation in, 58; salvation in, 107; sin in, 52; stewardship in, 69
Johnson, Elizabeth, 101n8
Jonah, Book of, 60
justice: animal pain and, 30; duty of, toward animals, 22; kingdom of God and, 134, 145; social, 150

kingdom of God, 4, 54, 62, 68, 110, 116, 132–38, 144
Klausner, Richard, 153–54

Last Battle, The (Lewis), 111
Last Judgment, 67, 104, 110
Latin Rite of the Catholic Church, 97
Laudato Si' (Francis), 4–5, 11, 15, 48, 51–52, 55, 66, 75–78, 88, 95–96, 157, 164. *See also* Francis, Pope
law: covenant and, 54; natural, 127, 130–31
Leibniz, Gottfried, 29
lemurs, 162
Leo X, Pope, 14–15
Leo XIII, Pope, 38
"Letter on Certain Questions Concerning Eschatology" (Congregation for the Doctrine of the Faith), 18–19
Lewis, C.S., 111
Limbo, 109
lions, 115
Liturgy of St. Basil, 97
love: of animals by Christ, 38–39; of animals by God, 20, 55; of animals by humans, 73; indirect, of animals by humans, 132; moral choice and, 35
Luke, Gospel of, 23, 54, 56, 73, 104, 133
Lumen Gentium (Vatican II), 50, 67, 96, 157, 165

magisterial views, 66–82
magpies, 34
Malebranche, Nicholas, 30
Manning, Henry Edward, 38
Mark, Gospel of, 54, 58, 60, 133
Marxism, 68
Mass, 97–98
Matthew, Gospel of, 37, 54, 56–57, 109, 133–34, 157
Maximus the Confessor, 36–37, 59
meat, 47, 80, 148–52
medicine. *See* experimentation, on animals; healing; vivisection
memory, preservation in divine, 74
mercy, 38, 134
"Message to the Stockholm Conference on the Human Environment" (Paul VI), 28–29
Methodists, 21
Middle Ages, 20
minority tradition, 36–39
mirror test, 34
Moral and Pastoral Theology, 22
moral choice, 35
moral duty, 132
Moral Philosophy, 22
Moral Principles and Medical Practice, 22
mourning, 35

naming, of pets, 73
natural law, 127, 130–31
nature, 20, 70, 105–7, 111–12
Neri, Philip, 38, 79, 147
Neuticles, 11
Newman, John Henry, 38

New Testament, 53–54, 57–58. *See also* *specific books*
Noah, 54, 60
nonhuman, as category, 33
nuisance animals, 137

Octogesima Adveniens (Paul VI), 28–29
octopuses, 114
Old Testament, 53–54, 57. *See also* *specific books*
Optatam Totius (Second Vatican Council), 133
orangutans, 33–34
original sin, 52

pain, 23, 30, 116, 128–29, 153. *See also* suffering
Paradiso (Dante), 111
particularity, of all creatures, 77
Paul, 54, 61
Paul VI, Pope, 9, 28–29
personality, 17–18, 74–75
personhood, 17–19
Peter, Second Book of, 58
pets, 5, 10–12, 73, 81. *See also* companion animals; dogs; domestication
Pets Evacuation and Transportation Standards (PETS), 10–11
pigs, 158n9
Pilgrim's Progress (Bunyan), 111
Pius IX, Pope, 21, 38, 40
Pius X, Pope, 38
plants, 13, 24, 47, 71–72, 75
Plato, 71
play, 113, 115–18
Poisson, Nicholas, 30
Polignac, Cardinal Melchoir de, 30
pollution, 28
Power and the Glory, The (Greene), 157
prayer, 6, 96–99, 108, 139
predation, 31, 113–15
primates, 33–34
protection, from animals, 137
Proverbs, Book of, 23
providence, 58–59, 79
Psalms, Book of, 58–59, 95, 119
pumas, 162
Puritans, 21

Quakers, 21

Ratzinger, Joseph, 49. *See also* Benedict XVI, Pope
reason: in animals, 35; in Aquinas, 12–13, 19, 24; Divine Reason, 95; virtue ethics and, 131
reasonableness, 37
redemption, 37, 39, 61, 63n9, 70, 73, 82, 98
Regan, Tom, 129
reindeer, 162
relational approach, 49
relationality, 145
relationships: among animals, 34–35, 74, 113–14; of animals with God, 112–13; in Francis, 165; as intended by God, 76; salvation and, 74–75; Trinity and, 88. *See also* companion animals; pets
research, on animals, 153–54. *See also* experimentation, on animals; vivisection
resurrection: of animals, 70–71, 77–78, 104; in Aquinas, 13, 17, 19, 24; body and, 15, 109–10; on Cathedral of Santa Maria Assunta, 104; of Christ, 73, 97, 113; cognition and, 16–17, 19; death and, 109–10; in Francis, 77–78; salvation and, 72; sentence and, 18
Revelation, Book of, 57
reward, heaven as, 108
Romans, Letter to, 37, 58, 60–61, 70
Royal Society for the Prevention of Cruelty to Animals (RSPCA), 21, 38
Ruland, Ludwig, 39

Salt, Henry S., 23
salvation: of animals, 48, 57–58, 62–63, 66–82; appropriation and, 92–93; in Balthasar, 91; Christ and, 2, 59, 68, 90–92, 94; cognition and, 71–73; as cosmic, 67; creation and, 143; death and, 72–73; Easter and, 100; Eucharist and, 96, 98; in Francis, 75–78; God and, 2; Holy Spirit and, 92–96; humans in, 96; in John Paul II, 107; prayer and, 96; preservation in divine memory as, 74; by proxy, 70–75, 164–65; redemption and, 82; relationships and, 74–75; replacement, 71; resurrection and, 72; as reward, 108; in Second Vatican Council, 71; sentience and, 72–73, 82; suffering and, 73; trinitarian theology and, 87–99; Trinity and, 90–92, 95, 165
salvation history, 2
Samuel, Second Book of, 53
science, 20–22, 27–28, 32–36, 40
sea cucumbers, 162–63
Second Coming, 4, 67, 110, 133
Second Vatican Council, 1, 4, 20, 24, 27–28; cosmic eschatology and, 40, 67–68; creation in, 71; environment and, 29; eschatology and, 82n1; *Gaudium et Spes,* 111–12; heaven in, 112; Holy Spirit in, 93; *Lumen Gentium,* 50, 67, 96, 157, 165; morality in, 133; *Optatam Totius,* 133; renewal in, 66; stewardship and, 50
self-awareness, 5, 17, 19, 33–34, 145
sentience, 5, 16–17, 72–73, 75, 82. *See also* cognition
sentient utilitarianism, 128–30
sin, 59, 98, 155, 165; animals as incapable of, 29–30, 96; animals as suffering for, 37; covenant and, 55; Fall and, 51–52; God's relationship to humanity and, 91–92; grace and, 106; meat-eating and, 47; nature and, 70; redemption and, 39; salvation and, 88; Trinity and, 91
Singer, Peter, 128
slaughterhouses, 149–50. *See also* factory farming
slavery, 61, 112
sociality, 34–35
solidarity, 52–53, 61, 96, 139
Son, the, 89–93, 100, 144. *See also* God; Jesus Christ
soul(s): all creatures as having, 13; of animals *vs.* humans, 13; in Aquinas, 13–14; in Boullier, 30–31; continuity and, 16–19; death and, 14; in Descartes, 30; immortality of, 13–15; as matter, 18
Spirit, the. *See* Holy Spirit
starlings, 114
stewardship, 49–51, 69, 79, 137–39
stimulus-response framework, 33
subjective awareness, 5, 16–17
subjectivity, 19, 24, 72–74, 145, 155–56, 164
suffering: of animals, 29–31, 80, 148; dignity and, 80, 132; for pleasure, 148; salvation and, 73. *See also* abuse, of animals
Summa Theologiae (Aquinas), 12, 52, 132

Tablet, The (weekly), 23, 38
technocratic paradigm, 155
theodicy, animal, 29–32, 40
Thomists, 20
tigers, 114
Timaeus (Plato), 71
tool use, 33–34
Trinity and trinitarian theology, 2, 89–96, 100; animal salvation and, 87–99; appropriation and, 92; in

Balthasar, 88–89, 91, 95; economic, 89–90; heaven and, 110; immanent, 89–90, 93–94; as mystery, 89; salvation and, 90–92, 95, 165

US Conference of Catholic Bishops (USCCB), 51, 58, 61, 99
utilitarianism, 127–30

Vatican II. *See* Second Vatican Council
veganism, 47
violence, 31, 113, 137, 148–50
virtue ethics, 127, 130–32, 149
vivisection, 21–22
vocation, 138–39

whales, 34, 113
White, Lynn, Jr., 27
wilderness, 136–37
wine, 97
wolves, 117
Wright, N. T., 63n9

Yarri, Donna, 156

Zechariah, Book of, 57, 60

ABOUT THE AUTHOR

Christopher Steck, SJ, is the Healey Family Distinguished Professor in Ethical Issues in the Department of Theology and Religious Studies at Georgetown University and editor in chief of *Theological Studies*. He is the author of numerous articles and books, including *All God's Animals: A Catholic Theological Framework for Animal Ethics* (GUP, 2019).